To the women in my life who made "Marathon Don" a possibility.

-Don Kern

Don Kern
1170 Oakburn Ave SE
Grand Rapids, MI 49546

Library of Congress Control Number: 2013943418

ISBN-10: 1620863685
ISBN-13: 9781620863688
CPSIA Code: PRB0713A

Book design by Joshua Taggert

Printed in the United States

www.mascotbooks.com

Acknowledgements

When climbing a mountain, the accomplishment should never be recognized until the climber returns safely to home base. The same applies to any adventure. These are the people who help me on my journeys, guide me along the way, and are there to share the joy at the end.

- Three of my "best friends," Paul Ruesch, Brent Weigner, and Shawn Sweet, my co-conspirators and fellow instigators.

- My own personal editor, Mike Zuidema, who asked me lots of questions and made me think and rewrite a lot of prose.

- My daughter, Katie, who gave me the excuse I needed to start running.

- The people back home, who help me stay grounded no matter how far away I get.

- The lovely Francine Robinson, who shares my home and my adventures and is always there at the end of the journey.

Table of Contents

and
the
adventure
continues....

An Ordinary Man's Extraordinary Quest to Set a World Record

Don Kern

MASCOT BOOKS

Foreword
by Michael Zuidema

The first time I met Don Kern, he gave me a man-hug. It didn't last long, maybe two or three seconds at the most, but it made a lasting impression. Then again, he had already made his mark long before I crossed the finish line of the inaugural Grand Rapids Marathon a sweaty, exhausted mess on October 31, 2004, when I was met with that quick embrace. I suspect I'm not alone in that sentiment.

I took up the sport of running shortly after graduating from college and, like anyone else, I suppose, started with 1-mile runs before graduating to 5Ks, 10Ks, 15Ks, and 25Ks. A marathon seemed like the next logical step.

So, in a rash and rather reckless move, I signed up for that first Grand Rapids Marathon. One problem: my longest training run—if you could even call it that—was a 25K (or, as I like to call it, 15.5 miles, since it seems to carry more significance with my metrically challenged friends) held the second weekend of May. In the five-plus months following that run, I managed to stay in decent shape, but never completed a 20-mile training run. Or another 15-miler. Or even a

10-miler. The longest distance I had completed was a 15K in mid-September. But as the Halloween date for the marathon loomed, I started to panic. What if I was in over my head? What if I irreversibly injured myself? What if I was left on the side of the road beside so many crumpled water cups, left to suffer alone in pain until I was swept aside with the rest of the trash?

It was this frame of mind that led me to first email Don Kern, the Grand Rapids Marathon race director, a mere week before the event. I did not expect him to reply, given the amount of work that must have been burying him then. Not only did he find time to email me, but he replied the very next day. And I'm glad he did.

My email consisted of one basic question: Given my pathetic level of training, should I switch from the full marathon to the half? I'm paraphrasing, but this is essentially what Don wrote back: "If you're in decent shape, go for the full. Sure, you'll be sore and tired and in pain, but once you cross the finish line, you'll have accomplished something you never thought possible. And no one will ever be able to take that away from you."

Naturally, he was right. Over the course of those 26.2 miles, I pushed past what I thought were my own limits and finished my first marathon. To this day, I consider it one of my proudest achievements, and I can confidently say I wouldn't have done it without that little extra push.

In recent years, I got to know Don a little better, both as a sports writer for *The Grand Rapids Press* and simply as another runner I chatted with over a beer. I learned about his passion for running, the marathons he's completed in all 50 states (twice)—not to mention 25 countries. I learned about the 109 consecutive months in which he ran at least one marathon, and his dogged pursuit of the world record for running a marathon on all seven continents in the shortest amount of time.

I also learned about Don's love for craft beer, climbing mountains, and finding the next great adventure. But the one revelation that stuck with me the most was discovering that his favorite thing to do every year is stand at the finish line of the Grand Rapids Marathon and give a quick hug or handshake to as many finishers as he can, whether they're finishing in less than three hours or more than seven. Because as much as Don likes testing his own limitations, he gleans even more satisfaction from seeing others surpass their own. It's one of many reasons why the Grand Rapids Marathon has become one of the top events if not in Michigan, then in the entire Midwest.

When Don asked me to help him with this book, I immediately signed on, but not because I wanted to relay his many globetrotting boondoggles, as entertaining as they may be. I wanted to help tell the story of a man who first found his own inspiration, then worked to help others find theirs. Hopefully, his tale will convince someone that limitations are made to be broken.

Like world records.

PREFACE

Before the Adventure Begins

I developed a pair of lists a while back: One is my "Life List." The other is a "Rule List." The first rule from the latter is this: "Everything I do is fun"—even if sometimes I don't realize it until a couple weeks later. Writing this book, however, has been fun all along the way.

In a lucky-for-me sequence of events, our local newspaper, *The Grand Rapids Press*, reorganized and updated their operations, and my good friend, sports writer Michael Zuidema—who was then known as "The Benchwarmer" for his snarky column and blog—decided to re-evaluate his employment situation. Mike and I had developed a rapport over the previous eight or nine years, ever since the first Grand Rapids Marathon was held in 2004. Since then, he had written numerous stories about the event, and a few about me as well. So, as I tried to figure out how to put pen to paper, Mike was available to help.

As we worked, Mike peppered me with questions. What motivated me? How did I feel? Why was any of this important? As a result, he made me wonder too. Why are things important to any of us? At the end of all this, we're just going to die, right? Somebody will rent a dumpster, park it in my front yard, and throw all my stuff in it. Morbid? Perhaps. Realistic? I think so.

Except that, well, things are important. Nearly everything that has ever lived is dead right now or will be soon enough. But somewhere along the way, certain stronger traits lived on as we progressed toward where we are today. DNA developed to make each successive generation stronger and better, and passing on our own strengths to the next generation is critical. Now, however, we're past just the basic DNA. In this next phase of human evolution, we'll contribute to the species by passing on our abilities, our hopes, our dreams, our examples—the things that can make all humans better, not just our direct descendants. I'll be the first to admit I'm just another fallible human being, but my goal, at the very least, is to help everyone I encounter become better in some way because we've met.

Let me share one important goal: I don't want you to read this and say, "Hey, that was a pretty darn good book." Hopefully, you will read this and feel compelled to do . . . something. Take action, book a trip, sign up for an adventure, and maybe add a few items to your own life list. If that happens, I'll consider it a success. Odds are you will too.

Help With the Perspective

It may seem at times as if this book is organized a little like a Quentin Tarantino film, where flashbacks fill in part of the story before it advances or the narrative advances in a nonlinear fashion. It worked in the 1994 classic film *Pulp Fiction*, and I hope it works here. Unlike a Quentin Tarantino film, though, nobody is shot and nobody's head gets chopped off. I'm saving that for the next book.

Since this isn't a typical autobiography covering everything from my birth to one foot in the grave, here's a quick background sketch of your fearless author:

> I was born on May 27, 1956, and grew up in Barryton, a small village of around 400 in central Michigan about twenty-some miles from Big Rapids. Our family wasn't rich, but I wouldn't have known it. We always had clothes to wear, food to eat, heat in the house, and toys for Mom to trip over. I had a brother and sister to play/fight with. I had grandparents to spend time with in the summers.

> I took piano lessons but never actually learned how to play. I'm not really compulsive, so I've never been addicted to cigarettes, alcohol, or drugs. I'm somewhat above average intelligence, so school was enough to keep me interested, but I didn't have to work real hard at it.

> My real dad died when I was 11 years old. Hey, maybe that's something in terms of overcoming adversity, but he was not really anyone I was ever close to, and by that time, I had a step-dad who later adopted us and treated us all OK. I had asthma when I was a kid, so I couldn't play baseball and all the sports I thought kids my age should do, but I was more of a scholar than an athlete anyway, so I didn't miss it much. In fact, I was one of the last guys to get picked for the team in gym class. So I suppose I was right where I wanted to be.

So there's no big dramatic setup here. Can just being a normal guy be the ticket? "Small Town Boy Makes Good." Overcomes humble beginnings, asthma, Father's death, Mother not making him practice piano enough, a few boiled dinners, and eating too many strawberries at Grandma's house. Now he runs a marathon every month, climbs a mountain every now and then, writes stories, and ran around the South Pole naked. Yeah, yeah. Who cares? How can this crap possibly be interesting?

In 1974, I graduated from Chippewa Hills High School, then attended Central Michigan University, earning a B.S. degree (which many thought appropriate until they found out what the B.S. actually stands for) with double majors in Mathematics and Speech & Dramatic Arts. Determined to be a teacher, I added a secondary education certificate.

Shortly after graduation, I married Nancy Portice and moved to Martin, another small village that sits about 20 miles north of Kalamazoo. It was there that we raised our children, Katie and Donald II, and later "adopted" a friend of the family, Lindsey Folk, a couple years before she finished high school, which I suppose made us an average American family of 2.3 kids. Give or take.

We lived in Martin until 2004, when Nancy and I decided to go in separate directions and I moved to Grand Rapids. That same year, I founded the Grand Rapids Marathon with the help of a few good friends. Around that time, Francine Robinson and I began spending a lot of time together. We still are. And the marathon is still running strong.

As far as my career is concerned, with the unusual combination of majors, I was a shoo-in for a teaching job in Martin for a math and speech teacher. After only one year, however, they decided to lay off a bunch of teachers, and that was just fine, since my temperament for being a constant disciplinarian just isn't that great, so teaching didn't agree very well. I tried selling life insurance for the summer, but that didn't go so well either; however, the financial field was attractive. Bill Coleman TV, one of the original rent-to-own companies, listed a job under "Credit/Finance," and I applied.

The job was pretty much just being a bill collector. However, Bill was on the verge of explosive growth at the beginning of the new industry, and he needed a computer guy. He gave me a key to the building so I could go into work thirty minutes early every day to complete a self-study tutorial on BASIC (computer language) programming. Another career was born, and after working for Coleman for six years as he opened 18 more stores, Qantel Business Computers offered me a job. A year later, they closed their office, and it was freelance work from then on. I still handle the occasional IT task, but the running/event management business occupies most of my time.

I've glossed over some of those early years not because they lack importance, but because so much of this book centers around 2007. That's when I made my first attempt at a world record and, well, a lot of really cool things subsequently happened.

Why did I keep searching for new stuff? I'm not sure I did. The "next thing" always seems to come along when I'm ready. I've come to believe there's a natural "flow" of things—my version of The Force, perhaps—that I somehow found and made a core piece of my philosophy.

Per Calvin (that's the six-year-old friend of Hobbes from the popular comic strip, not the noted French theologian and pastor): "They say the secret of success is being at the right place at the right time. But since you never know when the right time is going to be, I figure the trick is to find the right place and just hang around." I think maybe I've just mastered the art of standing in the right place because opportunities seem to run into me.

There you have it. If you get lost in time, come back here and find yourself.

Sometime along the way as you're reading this book, I hope you'll feel inspired to do something. Don't fight it. Stop at that point for a few minutes and go research a cool trip or add another item to your list. The words will still be here when you get back.

Prologue

The Life List

///

In August 1974, my mom, Julaine Kern, came into my room late one night and said something that changed my life forever. It was the summer between high school and college, and I'd spent the past three months working second shift at Evart Products on an instrument panel assembly line. My final shift ended at midnight on a late-August Friday, and the next morning I would set out on my 10-speed bike and ride the 85 miles from our house in Barryton, Michigan, to my grandma's house near Grand Ledge.

It was a way of challenging myself, the end of my childhood, and time to go out into the world. It was big and challenging, at a time when a young man (or an old boy) needs something big and challenging. I was hitting the sack on that hot August night, excited about my adventure the next morning, when Mom came in.

"Now, you know you won't be able to ride all the way to Grand Ledge, so don't be afraid to call your grandma and have her come pick you up."

Whether Mom was using reverse psychology, or her paradigms about my abilities had her believing what she had just said, remains a mystery. But at the end of her statement, something clicked in my brain. It was one of those instant changes in attitude and outlook where things would never be the same. I've since defined those moments as "Marathon Minutes." What's a marathon minute? It's that sudden realization that there's more strength in you than you thought there was. It's that minute when you dig down deep and grab that extra "something" that allows you to push on through the finish line. It's that minute that leaves you feeling stronger, happier, and healthier than you were in the minute before.

It was at that particular moment I decided I would die peddling my bicycle before I would stop to call Grandma. At 6:30 the next morning, the pedals on my Raleigh Record started turning, heading south on M-66, beginning the biggest physical challenge of my young life.

After nearly 50 miles, rolling into downtown Ionia seemed easy, and a quart of root beer from A&W hit the spot. Soon, however, I would have to pay for the easy roll into town. Ionia is in the Grand River valley, and when I pedaled up out of the valley heading out the south end of town, my legs protested loudly. Better than 3 miles of steady climbing put a few doubts in my mind. I caught myself scanning oncoming traffic, thinking maybe one of the cars would be Grandma and Grandpa, that perhaps Mom had sent them to look for me.

Even with the discouragement growing during that toughest part of the trip, every pedal stroke moved me a few feet closer to my goal. After what seemed like forever, the two wheels found level ground. Gravity was no longer the enemy. The final third of the trip was underway. 12 miles from Grandma's house, turning east onto M-43 put the wind at my back, a surprising push that made the final miles the fastest and easiest of the trip.

I turned into the yard, my momentum and excitement carrying me up the hill to the back door. Grandma, who had been half-expecting to hear my voice on the phone, was surprised to see me in person as I walked into the house just before 3 p.m. The trip took over eight hours, including several breaks and a short nap on the side of the road. But it was done!

Mom hasn't given me any reason to think she doubts my abilities since then. The most significant lesson of that day was about personal limits. *I don't have any.*

When I actually started my life list is uncertain, but that bike ride would have been worthy of it. Long before hearing of the concept, the list was taking root. Later, the concept of a life list would gel, coming together to propel me through my own life of adventure. The feeling of accomplishment that day in 1974 helped me realize a person can take control of life and accomplish almost anything.

It had been more than ten years since that bout of pneumonia a month or so before my eighth birthday had weakened my lungs. I spent much of that time fighting for air instead of playing Little League or engaging in other athletic endeavors. Even before that, I was one of the "brainy kids" as opposed to the "jocks," every bit as content with reading as playing outside. I spent lots of time "keeping my own counsel," plotting and scheming, and dreaming about the future. Like a lot of kids, I imagined myself "bigger than life," inspired by popular television shows like *Superman*, *Batman*, and later, *Kung Fu*. Non-fiction was pretty heroic then too, with John Glenn going into space and Neil Armstrong and Buzz Aldrin landing on the moon, setting new standards of adventure and exploration. Maybe I wasn't an athlete, but the vision of me doing amazing things became part of my thought process.

In 1972, not long after our family got its first color television, we watched the Munich Olympics. The endurance, gracefulness, and strength planted a seed in my young mind that would take more than two decades to sprout. Around that same time, I saw someone on a TV show about the South Pole walk "around the world" and saw myself there. The List, not yet a formal document, was growing.

While The List wouldn't come into being for a while, I was always "a man with a plan." Living in the future was part of me, and there were always thoughts in the back of my mind that I would be rich and famous, accomplish great things, set the world on fire.

My real dad worked in the feed mill. Mom was a clerk at the drug store. After Mom and Dad divorced, Mom remarried and went to work for Evart Products, and my new dad was a custodian at Ferris State University in nearby Big Rapids. No silver spoons in my mouth. It didn't matter. Growing up, the earliest discussions my mom had with me about education involved me going to college someday. So, despite the fact that no one in our family had ever been to college, it never occurred to me that I wouldn't go.

After graduating high school, I set off to get my life started. Planning to become a teacher and being a fairly good student, college proved to be no problem. I worked my way through Central Michigan University in only three years, going to summer sessions and taking heavy class loads. Just before my twenty-first birthday, I graduated from CMU and married Nancy that summer. Before I turned twenty-two, our daughter Katie was born. The impatience of youth had a pretty firm grip. The whole world was waiting.

During my early adulthood, Nightingale Conant, a company specializing in motivational and self-improvement programs, had a deal where one could sample their tape programs free for thirty days before buying them. With a half-hour commute to work, there was plenty of time to listen to motivational programs that convinced me of the importance of setting goals. Most people my age spent that time listening to music on the radio; I spent it furthering ambitions for the future.

In the early 1990s, motivational speaker Michael Wickett spoke in Grand Rapids. He related the story of John Goddard who, at the young age of 15, created a "Life List" of 127 goals and used that list to organize his life into a series of adventures. Goddard had inspired goal setters for decades.

Wickett expounded on the importance of spending enough time to come up with at least 100 goals. Spending that much time and thought causes one's life to move in a direction and develop a sense of purpose. The important things become clear.

Teenage years were long past, and the age of computers and spreadsheets arrived. I had no more time to waste. I sat in front of my computer, opened a new spreadsheet file in a version of Microsoft Office that I loaded off 3.5-inch floppy disks, and assembled my ambitions, dreams, and goals into one place.

The results were interesting. Even inspiring. It's amazing what developed along the way. Things popped into mind that had never occurred to me. Before many days had passed, the list had grown long. Just having the list was motivational. Even though I created the life list, it took on a life of its own, guiding me in directions I had unknowingly chosen.

Creating a life list may be the closest thing any of us will ever get to creating life itself. (That sexual reproduction thing is a process we had nothing to do with—it was here long before we were.) As the list grew, it seemed to act more and more like a living organism. The goals meshed together, complementing one another, pulling me along with them. I gave it life, and now it gives me life.

My life list is not a fixed list like Goddard had. Rather, I never let it shrink below a hundred items. Every year, I check a few items and add a few more. Some of the completed items include the following:

- Run a marathon.
- Complete an Ironman-distance triathlon.
- Visit Macchu Picchu.
- Visit all fifty States.
- Run marathons on seven continents.

- See the Harlem Globetrotters.
- Go kayaking in the ocean.
- See the Acropolis.
- Watch a total lunar eclipse.
- Climb Mt. Kilimanjaro.

Those are just a few things, but many remain to be accomplished, such as the following:

- Run with the bulls in Pamplona.
- Go cage diving with Great White Sharks.
- Sit in a hot spring in Yellowstone in the winter.
- Kiss the Blarney Stone.
- Run on the Great Wall of China.
- Go fishing in Alaska.
- See grizzly bears in the wild.

And many, many others, including…

Set a world record?

One fateful day in 2006, as I sat in a bagel shop on my way to a client site to do some regular work as a computer programmer/consultant, I found a copy of the *Guinness Book of World Records*. Skimming through the pages, I happened upon something that would change the course of my life for at least the following six years. My direction was clear from that moment. There was no doubt what I needed to do.

For a later-in-life, former-asthmatic runner, setting a world record could be difficult. I'm not very fast. I'm not tall, I'm not short, I'm not fat, and I'm not skinny. I lack the patience to spend 32 years growing my fingernails, hair, or other body parts. Still, I needed to do something at world record pace. My world. My record. My pace.

Fortunately, as it turns out, marathons are my thing.

Chapter 1

Running is Hard

Running is hard. At least that's what I thought as I grew out of childhood and my lungs improved. Still, running 2 miles would leave me sore for a few days, and the next thing you knew, I *wasn't* in the habit of running. I liked the idea of being athletic. But I wasn't. So I spent my extra-curricular time in theater, debate, and forensics. At school sporting events, I was a spectator.

As a young adult in college, then later as my kids grew and maybe a couple of other times, I tried to run. Every time I'd go out, though, my legs hurt, so I wouldn't run again for a while. Life faded back to what it was before, and running wasn't a part of it.

Until I found the secret.

At the beginning of spring in 1994, my daughter Katie joined the high school track team at Martin High School. While I had tried to stay in shape, play racquetball, and do some aerobic training on the machines at the health club, my running was limited to a mile at a time on the treadmill. Still, it seemed like running was important. After all, what sport doesn't include running?

One evening before official practices started, Katie and I walked up to the high school track and decided to do 2 miles. Run, walk, whatever, just get through it. I jogged around the track, and by keeping the pace slow and my feet moving forward, I made a discovery. *I could go slow and easy* and run 2 miles without stopping and without pain. Aha!

One time, I listened to a friend talk with some enthusiasm about a 10K race that actually took place in the town of Martin, where I lived at the time. I remember thinking that running over 6 miles would be a pretty good accomplishment. After that initial run with Katie, suddenly the desire to run was rekindled. Maybe 10K would be possible someday.

As track season progressed, I spent time on the roads with both my kids, going at a slow pace but lengthening the runs a little more all the time. By May, I could run over 6 miles, and by the end of summer, I was ready to make the jump. On Labor Day that year, I added the first of a large collection of running T-shirts to my wardrobe. That shirt came from the Scenic Emmet Challenge 10K in Battle Creek. It was tough, with part of it on trails, and because I was one of the slower runners, there was a stretch where I wasn't sure I was on course because I couldn't see any runners ahead of me. Still, I got through that first 10K in a little over an hour.

I've heard it said that one could get addicted to cocaine after the very first dose. Want to know something else? You can get addicted to T-shirts after the very first road race.

What followed over the next year was a series of moments that would eventually turn a non-running computer guy into someone who would eventually be tagged with the nickname "Marathon Don."

The normal lull of winter (you can't run in the snow, can you?) sent me back indoors for very short runs on the treadmill. But when the weather turned nice, spring fever hit, and I went back out onto the roads. That March, my whole family signed up for the Maple Syrup Run 5K in Ada, Michigan. It was a fun event followed by a pancake breakfast.

Shortly thereafter, I met a neighbor a block over from my house in Martin, Michigan. Joe Hulsebus and I stood in his front yard talking about running, since he had seen me out on the roads a few times. Joe had a great attitude toward running and told me about the Fifth Third River Bank Run 25K, one of the largest road events in West Michigan. His vivid description got me excited as well, and I decided to sign up and give it a try.

On Mother's Day weekend, having trained only to a long run of 15K two weeks before at the Borgess Run for the Health of It in Kalamazoo, I took the challenge of running 25 kilometers (about 15.5 miles). It was a long, slow day, but at the end, I had a finisher's medal and a new goal.

A few miles before a volunteer placed the medal around my neck, we were running along the Grand River near the 7-mile mark at the far end of Indian Mounds Road. I listened as a couple not-too-small guys discussed training for a marathon. Before we reached mile 8, running a marathon that fall seemed like a reasonable thing to do. By mile 9, despite the fact that I had never even thought about running a marathon before, I was determined to run a marathon that fall. So as I waited for my sore legs to feel better after the 25K, I formulated a training plan for that fall, targeting the Columbus Marathon on November 12.

The training continued. One day that summer, I was home for lunch, eating a bowl of chili and reading the current issue of *Runner's World* magazine, when I found an upside-down article. It wasn't a mistake; it was a story about the first Antarctica Marathon, which was held on January 28, 1995, and was the brainchild of Thom Gilligan, owner of Marathon Tours and Travel in Boston. Before even finishing the article, I put the magazine down and called Marathon Tours in Boston to sign up for the next running in 1997. No discussion. No debate. I just knew. I had traveled to six continents on previous trips, but here was my chance to travel to the seventh, and run a marathon too.

The other buzz in the running world at that time was the 100th running of the Boston Marathon to come in 1996. For one-time only, runners could enter a special "Open Division" by lottery, allowing those of us not fast enough to run a qualifying time an opportunity to run the world's most famous marathon. Knowing my dismal chance of qualifying, I put my entry in the hat.

My "Life List" was growing longer as my legs were growing stronger.

As my training progressed, my fall schedule changed as well, so instead of running my first marathon in Columbus, I went to Chicago for the LaSalle Banks Chicago Marathon on October 15. It was what I wanted to do anyway, since I had a free place to stay with a college buddy, Mike Schwartz. Mike had run a marathon when we were 28 and had never let me forget about it.

That summer, I also joined the Dead Runners Society, an Internet mailing list filled with people from all over the world who love to run. That was where I first heard about the Midnight Sun Marathon in Tromso, Norway. My wife Nancy's brother, Bob, lived near Oslo, and we had talked about a family vacation there at some point. We decided to schedule it around the marathon so I could run north of the Arctic Circle on July 6, 1996.

Experienced runners would have questioned the wisdom of entering multiple marathons before I had even completed one. Fortunately, I wasn't an experienced runner. Like the bike ride to my grandma's house a couple decades earlier, it didn't occur to me that a slightly "over the top" goal was anything unreasonable.

So, before running my first marathon, I had apparently succumbed to marathon fever, signed up for four marathons, and was planning a fifth.

On October 10, 1995, five days before running my first marathon in Chicago, the second drawing for the 100th Boston became my lucky day. I was going to Boston.

Five marathons were on the schedule. Yet TRSKAMD (The Runner Subsequently Known As Marathon Don) had yet to conquer his first 26.2-mile distance. Anyone who has ever run a marathon will tell you it's a long run and never a certainty. Call it naiveté, blissful ignorance, or just plain stupidity, but I was doing it anyway.

Chapter 2

Marathons on Seven Continents

Between March 1994 and May 1995, my transition from non-runner to runner was complete. The subsequent discovery of adventures associated with marathons turned running from a healthful hobby into a lifestyle. On October 15, 1995, a journey that continues to this day began in Chicago, Illinois.

North America: United States, Chicago—October 1995

It was a day of excitement, anticipation, and awe. Even checking in the day before the marathon at the expo, visiting the booths, and meeting people in the running business, it was plain I was where I wanted to be. Dead Runners Society members had arranged to meet there for an encounter, and it was there I met Aziz Uras, who would be my running companion for the first 16 miles the next day. (Seventeen years later, we still run into each other on the marathon circuit occasionally.) Samuel Adams Brewing was a sponsor, and that day was also my first taste of Cherry Wheat. Perhaps it was the first microbrew in my "beer career."

I spent the night before the marathon with my college buddy Mike Schwartz. Early Sunday morning, I left his place in Skokie to head downtown. The starting line was a madhouse, and more runners than I imagined even existed were there to test their limits and see if 26.2 miles was possible.

Before running that first marathon, while running many miles alone through the farm country around Martin, Michigan, I developed the idea that anyone who can run 26.2 miles can do anything. It was finally time to find out if that was true, if my training was enough. Even with over 11,000 runners in the starting corral, I somehow ran into Aziz again, and we ran together all the way to mile 16. Aziz posted in his report on the Dead Runners Society mailing list the next day, "Don stayed on pace, and I went on ahead." The truth is, a couple pretty girls in hot pink outfits caught up with us, and he found their company preferable to mine. Also, it was more like *he* stayed on pace and I faded. Anyway, I would have done the same thing—the girls were pretty.

Around 18 miles, I picked up another running partner named Nancy. Together we worked the course, best friends for around an hour or so. As we passed the 20-mile mark, she surpassed her personal record distance. At 22 miles, I surpassed mine. At the turn toward the finish near 23 miles, her sister and Schwartz were both waiting, so we parted ways and ran with our respective support person. Visualizing the finish line would cause me to get choked up, so I just listened to Mike talk (perhaps his best talent) and plugged on past the 24 and 25-mile markers. After five hours and seven minutes of forward motion, I was still aware enough to make sure the finish line photographers had a clear view of me as I crossed the finish line. My first marathon finish line. My first marathon finisher medal. Old limits were gone. I had run

26.2 miles. I could do anything.

Four weeks later, the Columbus Marathon was the setting for my second marathon finish, and then in April it was off to Boston, where a world record was set for the highest number of confirmed finishers at a marathon. It turned out to be my first appearance in the *Guinness Book of World Records*. Well, me and 38,705 of my closest friends, anyway.

Boston was everything I had hoped, a celebration of the sport in one of the most historic cities in our nation. The people of Islam make a pilgrimage to Mecca once in their lifetimes. For marathon runners, Mecca is Boston. I had made my pilgrimage. But my adventures were only beginning.

Chicago, Columbus, and Boston were complete. In May, I ran the Bayshore Marathon in Traverse City, Michigan, and finished in under five hours. A week later, because it was close to home, the Sunburst Marathon in South Bend, Indiana, became marathon number five. The next month would start my international marathon quest.

Europe: Tromso, Norway—July 1996

On July 5, 1996, an unexpected American arrived at the airport in Tromso, Norway, 69-degrees 40-minutes North latitude, more than 200 miles north of the Arctic Circle.

Flying by the seat of my pants is my favorite way to go most of the time, so it didn't bother me that I hadn't registered for this particular marathon ahead of time. Spending the extra time and money on an international funds draft (i.e., a money order in Norwegian funds) didn't appeal to me. Late registration on site would have to do. At the airport, I ran into a guy named Peter who saw I was wearing a marathon shirt and thought I was one of the people he was there to pick up. I wasn't. We located the two runners he was looking for, and he gave us all a ride into town. By that afternoon, Peter had told a friend at the newspaper about me, and the *Tromso Daily News* interviewed me. "American shows up with no entry and no reservations to run the marathon." Nice human-interest story, I suppose. The newspaper quoted me in Norwegian, and I don't even speak Norwegian.

The next night at 10 p.m., we started the Midnight Sun Marathon, running past midnight to the early hours of the morning. "Hy-ah, hy-ah, hy-ah," the spectators shouted as we ran by, a different cheer than I had ever heard. In the last kilometer, a young man encouraged me as I ran by, but when he saw I didn't understand, he took off his hat and said, "My hat is off to you." A little after 3 a.m., my body clock was very confused, but my first international marathon was in the books.

That marathon in Tromso was my sixth marathon, my first in Chicago only eight months earlier. The shirts, the finisher medals, and the ground-level tours of the cities had me hooked. My small collection of medals and cool shirts grew, and I loved what I was doing. Before I left for Antarctica in February 1997, the total would increase by another three: the Fox Cities Marathon in Appleton, Wisconsin; my second Chicago Marathon, and Disney World in January 1997.

Antarctica: King George Island, off the Coast of the Antarctic Peninsula—February 1997

At the Miami International Airport, a group of strangers-soon-to-be-friends identified one another by our various marathon shirts as we congregated for the flight to Buenos Aires, en route to Antarctica. That was the day I met John Bozung, from Orem, Utah, who was on a mission to run all seven continents that year. Antarctica would be my third continent. Friends I had met only minutes before could already hear the wheels in my head turning.

The greatest part of going on a trip such as this is the friendships we make along the way. Being cooped up on a ship with adventure-minded people for over a week builds relationships in a hurry. It's also a little dangerous, because drinking coffee and swapping stories in the morning can rapidly add a half-dozen items to your life list.

After spending a couple very enjoyable days in Buenos Aires (perhaps the best girl-watching city in the world), we flew south to Ushuaia, the world's southernmost city, where we would board the *Akademik Ioffe* for the trip to the White Continent. The trip across the Drake Passage can be one of the roughest crossings in the world, with the ocean currents squeezing in between South America and the Antarctic Peninsula. Fortunately, I had only a couple bouts of seasickness on the way down. After arriving in Antarctic waters, however, the seas calmed, and it was very pleasant living on the *Ioffe*.

The *Akademik Vavilov* arrived a day before with the race staff who had gone ashore and set up the course. On race morning, February 17, we dressed for running and got ready to board the Zodiac boats for the short shuttle to King George Island, but we got some bad news. The people on the *Vavilov* had managed to get in to shore, but because we were positioned a little farther out and the winds were picking up, the captain decided we shouldn't risk getting off the ship. As the runners from the *Vavilov* waited for the start, we were helpless on the *Ioffe*. Finally, the crew gave up and fed us lunch, and the Antarctica Marathon started without us.

As we ate, however, the ship started to move. The captain managed to reposition our ship a little closer to shore in a slightly more sheltered area. As we finished our meal, the announcement came over the speakers: "Get dressed. We're going to run a marathon." The dining hall emptied in a hurry, and we were soon on Zodiac boats headed for shore. Around two hours after our colleagues from the *Vavilov* had begun the marathon, we started "wave 2." With stomachs full of empanadas and hearts full of joy, we were running a marathon in Antarctica.

The course started off through a patch of shoe-sucking mud that would worsen as the day went on. It included hills, glacial runoff, mud, rocks, and a stretch up and down a glacier as we ran an out-and-back section from Bellingshausen (the Russian research base) through Artigas (the Uruguayan base) and then back to the center, where we went out past a Chilean base to the Great Wall Chinese base. Along the way, a couple chinstrap penguins provided some black and white "crowd support."

The mud, trampled by a few hundred feet, was waiting for us as we repeated the course a second time. I barely caught myself before putting a sock into the mud a step after it had swallowed my shoe. The weariness felt during the later miles made the hills more difficult the second time, and the wind seemed to pick up a bit. On my second trip out to the Great Wall, running with travel companions Bob Platt and Sarann Mock from Cincinnati, we found ourselves between a fur seal and the water. He made it very plain that he wasn't happy about it, chasing us until he knew we were out of his territory.

When all the *Ioffe* dwellers had finished their marathon, the times of the two heats were combined and the results posted, and the second ever Antarctica Marathon—"The Last Marathon," as it is called—was completed, in spite of the tense moments earlier in the day.

We spent the next few days visiting penguin rookeries, cruising around icebergs, seeing seals and glaciers, and enjoying the magnificent Antarctic scenery. I've heard it said that more people go through the turnstiles of Disney World in a day than have traveled to Antarctica in all of history. It was truly a privilege to be there.

The trip back across the Drake Passage was a little rougher, and a good deal of the trip was spent lying in my bunk, catching up on some reading while keeping my queasy stomach under control.

South America: Caracas, Venezuela—July 1997

After that successful trip to Antarctica, I set out to locate marathons on other continents, but South America was proving to be elusive. I sent an email to my buddy Cliff Jennings, one of the staff at Marathon Tours, to ask for suggestions. A few minutes later, he replied, telling me about a trip they were planning to Caracas, Venezuela, that summer. The next email went to Paul Ruesch, a shipmate from the Antarctica trip who was destined to become one of my best friends. The subject line was, "You want to have some fun?" I told him I needed a roommate. He replied less than an hour later: "I just emailed Cliff and told him I'm going."

Back on the *Ioffe*, Paul and I spent a bit of time together and got along well. He credits me for making him realize, as a result of inviting him on this trip, that you could just drop everything and go on an adventure on short notice. In fact, this trip is probably where I learned it too.

Paul remembers sitting at a table in Antarctica marveling at the marathon tales other runners had conquered. At the time, it was only his third marathon and by far the most extreme. Little did he know what lay ahead.

"I remember thinking these people were completely crazy," Paul recalled. "Don and I connected later since we were both from the Midwest. We started talking, and that's when I learned more about him, his marathon experiences, and his plans. He struck me as very down-to-earth in that he didn't seem impressed at all with himself or what he was doing, just a normal guy running here and there because he thought it was fun."

The group left early on the morning of July 18, and the twenty or so of us partied that night in Caracas. The next day was reserved for tours, followed by a reception for international runners on Saturday night. On Sunday, we ran the Maratón Libertador on a blistering hot day only a couple degrees away from the Equator. The streets of Caracas were open to traffic, and I frequently found myself struggling to keep the person in front of me in sight so I wouldn't lose the course.

After a long, hot run through the Venezuelan capitol, the finish line appeared over a kilometer in the distance at the far end of the Paseo de Los Proceres. Sunday night was a post-race celebration party, and the next morning, the bus took us to the airport. By Monday night, I was sleeping in my own bed back in Martin, Michigan. A four-day weekend and a marathon in South America. Only three more continents to go.

Asia: Tiberias, Israel—January 1998

On January 1, 1998, I started the New Year with the annual 4-mile Resolution Run in East Grand Rapids, then showered at the school locker room and left for the airport and a trip to Israel.

The previous summer, I had contacted Isram Tours and Travel to see if they could organize a trip, and before an hour had passed, their agent Dubi Leshem had lined up a ten-day tour that included trips through Old Jerusalem, New Jerusalem, along the Dead Sea to Masada and Qumran, Bethlehem, Tel Aviv, and several other sites throughout Israel. In the middle of all that was the Tiberias Marathon by the Sea of Galilee. Three of my companions from the Antarctica Marathon joined me on that trip, Art Blume and Roy and Virginia Farneman.

On Wednesday evening, our personal guide Moshe dropped us off in Tiberias for the marathon. It rained all night, and by morning, some of the downtown streets were flooded near the starting line. We had to pick our way around the newly formed streams that crossed the streets during the first couple kilometers, but it had stopped raining and was just clouded over. We continued south and then east toward the southernmost point of the lake, crossing a small bridge over the tiny stream that forms the very beginning of the Jordan River, coming out of the sea and heading south. We continued up the east side of the Sea, with the Golan Heights rising in the distance to the east. As we reached the halfway point and turned around to head back, we heard automatic gunfire off in the distance, hopefully from a practice range.

I finished in a personal record time of 4:32. It was a great trip, adding a lot of perspective to the stories I grew up with in Sunday school. Virginia later became the first woman, and thus the first women's world record holder, to complete all seven continents. Only two more continents would complete my circuit.

Africa: Moshe, Tanzania—June 1998

While on the phone with another friend from that first Antarctic trip, Mark Huckenpahler, he told me about the Mount Kilimanjaro Marathon. Marie Frances, a producer from Bethesda, Maryland, organized the event in June. One look at Marie and you could tell she wasn't an athlete. She describes herself as an Italian Mama, all soft and cuddly. But she loves what she does. I recruited a few more people to go along as well, including my wife Nancy, my mom Julaine, and my son Donald II. We spent a couple days in Paris on the way, climbing the Eiffel Tower, taking in the Louvre and the Cathedral of Notre Dame, and shopping along the Champs-Élysées.

We flew into Nairobi, Kenya and took a long overnight bus ride to Arusha, Tanzania, where we spent the day before continuing on to Moshe. During the next four days, half the group, including Donald and me, climbed Mount Kilimanjaro while Nancy and Mom went on safari to the Serengeti with the others.

It was a fascinating adventure, as the climb took us through many climates on our way to Africa's summit. A jungle hike on the first day was followed by a very rainy second day, climbing through a foggy mist to Horombo camp. Spectacular night skies with constellations unfamiliar to those of us from the northern hemisphere gave way to something even more breathtaking the next morning. As we stepped out of our A-frame huts, we found ourselves in a city above the clouds. The mist we hiked through the previous day was actually a blanket of soft, fluffy clouds that blocked out the world below in every direction. The third day of our climb took us through an alpine desert to Kibo camp at 15,500 feet to rest for a short night before making our summit attempt.

Shortly after midnight, we woke to start the final push. From the roof of Africa, Uhuru Peak, the uppermost of Kilimanjaro's three summits, we watched the sun rise over the African Continent. A bet between father and son over who would puke first due to altitude sickness ended in a tie, with both of us somehow managing to avoid such unpleasantries.

We descended through scree fields to Kibo camp, rested up a bit, and continued to Horombo to spend the night. The next day, we hiked all the way back to the bottom. The double-digit miles of irregular downhill hiking caused a lot of discomfort in the quads as we made our way down Africa's highest mountain.

We were supposed to have a rest day in between, but instead, we held the marathon the very next day in Moshe, with legs still sore from descending the final 15 miles the previous day. The marathon was the least-inspiring part of the trip, a four-loop course around the little town of Moshe. The real highlight was standing with my son on the highest point of the African Continent.

Not only an African marathon, I now had a continental high point checked off my life list. Was another hobby in the works? Maybe. But there was only one continent left.

Oceania: Adelaide, South Australia—August 1998

Shortly after arriving home, one of my business investments paid off, so instead of waiting any longer, Nancy and I booked a trip to Australia to finish the seven continents. We flew into Sydney and spent a few days touring that part of the country before flying to Adelaide for number seven.

Adelaide is a beautiful city, notable because unlike most large cities, it was planned before it was built. The downtown consists of wide streets and great shopping districts. In a huge ring of green surrounding the town are all the parks, football ovals, rugby fields, golf courses, etc. Outside of that are the suburbs.

The marathon registration form had included a place to put some press information, and finishing the seven continents seemed press-worthy to someone at the race site, who had apparently alerted the hotel to keep an eye out for me. No more than a few minutes after checking in at the Grosvenor Hotel, a reporter called from the local paper to interview me about finishing my seventh continent. Out of seven continents, I made the local papers in two of them. Not bad for a small-town kid.

The most unique feature of this marathon (from an American perspective) was the way they marked the kilometers, counting down instead of up. After 195 meters, we were at the 42-kilometer mark, and the numbers counted down. The half-marathon and 10K used the same markers, so only one set was needed for all the races. Much of the race was run around the green spaces that surrounded the central city, resulting in a beautiful course. After running for nearly four and a half hours, I raised seven fingers above my head and crossed the finish line on August 9, 1998, becoming the 14th person in the world to run marathons on all seven continents.

The time span between my first international marathon in Norway and the finish of the seven continents was 764 days. That's just a little over two years. Those two years had been a whirlwind of travel, and a great education on life around the world. There were new friends for life who would play recurring parts in my story. It was an awesome feeling, resting on my laurels. But laurels get pretty uncomfortable in a fairly short time. Gotta get up and do something else.

Meanwhile, an entry in the *Guinness Book of World Records* had been established in 1997 by Hajime Nishi of Japan, as he completed marathons on seven continents in 168 days. A new record category was established—"The Fastest Time to Run a Marathon on Each of the Seven Continents"—when he made his submission. He wasn't the first to complete the seven continents, so technically he broke someone else's record, but he was the first to submit it. The stage was set.

Chapter 3

One for the Record Books

I first came upon the *Guinness Book of World Records* during my freshman year at Chippewa Hills High School in Remus, Michigan. Every few weeks in college preparatory English class came the opportunity to order books from the Scholastic Book Club. While looking at Scholastic's flyer one fall day in 1970, I was intrigued by the description of a book that would have a yet unknown effect on my life. It looked interesting, and soon I decided to spend $1.25 and order a copy.

According to the Guinness website, the history of the Guinness World Records dates back to 1951 Ireland, where Sir Hugh Beaver, then the managing director of the Guinness Brewery, asked a simple question: What was Europe's fastest game bird? The query sparked a heated argument, but an answer could not be found after an exhaustive search of the host's reference library. Beaver realized that similar questions must have been going unanswered in other regions of the world, so he set about to compile the definitive collection of superlative facts with the help of Norris and Ross McWhirter, fact-finding twins from London. On August 27, 1955, the first edition of the Guinness Book of Records was published. By Christmas, it was Britain's No. 1 bestseller.

By the fall of 1970, when my copy arrived, it was called the *Guinness Book of World Records*. My new Bantam Books edition was a 4" x 7" paperback volume a little over an inch thick. As I scoured the small print and black-and-white pictures, many items seemed bigger than life. But there were also many things a normal person like me might be able to accomplish one day. Not being an Olympic caliber athlete or a morbidly obese motorcycle-riding twin, it would take some creativity. Sitting on a pole, jumping on a pogo stick, making a gigantic ball of aluminum foil—it didn't matter. Loads of tasks seemed plausible at the time. I spent way too much of Bob Loesch's class time dreaming of the fame a small-town kid would garner for being in the book. (Bob was my favorite teacher in high school and remains a good friend to this day.)

The idea of doing something that was the biggest, best, or most amazing in any given field was outside the realm of possibility for most people, me included. But I was young and full of dreams. It was an age of possibilities. Men were landing on the moon, the Detroit Tigers had recently won the World Series, and the computer age was almost upon us. Great things were happening. The world was filled with opportunity, and I wanted to join in. I often wondered, "What can I do, what will I ever do, better than anyone else in the world?" I did not expect to make an Olympic team or play on a world championship team, so I filed the question under "Things I Just Have to Live With." Once in a while, however, it would return to my consciousness. Someday the issue would have to be addressed.

I never bought another copy of the *Guinness Book of World Records*, but I'd see a copy here and there over the years. Through the decades, the book evolved into the glossy, picture-filled "coffee table" volume it's become in the 21st century. I still enjoyed flipping through the pages, reading about the wild, wonderful, and off-the-wall marks that ordinary people were accomplishing at a rapid pace. Someday....

Then one day in early 2006, while eating a cranberry-walnut bagel and drinking coffee at the Bagel Beanery just south of Grand Rapids, I found the latest issue of The Book. There, somewhere amid photographs of the world's largest twins and the longest set of fingernails, I happened upon something that caught my interest:

MARATHON ON EACH CONTINENT - MEN

Tim Rogers (UK) completed a marathon on each of the seven continents in 99 days between February 13 and May 23, 1999.

Tim began with the Antarctica Marathon on King George Island and subsequently visited the U.S., South Africa, France, Brazil, and Hong Kong before finishing in Huntly, New Zealand.

I'm pretty sure the Bagel Beanery brightened, either from the light bulb above my head or the big smile on my face, because that was the moment, I knew.

I could break a **world record.**

Chapter 4

Around the World in 35 Days

Between October 15, 1995, and August 8, 1998, a period of over a thousand days, I became the fourteenth person to run marathons on all seven continents. (The first time it was possible to run a marathon in Antarctica was 1995, so the number of people who could possibly have run a marathon on seven continents was fairly easy to document.) After that fateful day in the Bagel Beanery, the next world tour would be just a bit more intense. Much of 2006 was spent plotting a way to do it in fewer than 99 days.

Because the trip was so enjoyable in 1997, I had signed up to run The Last Marathon with Marathon Tours again in 2007. It looked like a race would be held in Ushuaia, Argentina, only a couple days after we landed there on the return trip from the White Continent of Antarctica. That would be two continents on that trip in only a little over a week.

Whether it's a blessing or a curse is hard to tell, but when my brain grabs hold of an idea like that, there's no way to turn it off. My Internet connection was humming as the search for international marathons commenced, and the plot to run the seven continents in under 99 days thickened. Surprisingly, that task proved quite easy, so I altered the plan even more to figure out exactly how fast it could be done. I checked race calendars from around the world to search for the right combination of marathons that would put my name in the record book.

On the Guinness website, I registered my intentions and got the criteria for their documentation. For this particular record, all marathons needed to be officially organized events—not just individual runs contrived for the sole purpose of this record. So finding actual races on the continents would be my next task.

Finding a marathon to run on every continent is a treasure hunt in itself. The U.S. and Canada are easy because most are listed on the Marathon Guide's website. It's a good place to begin with international marathons as well, but only a start, as other countries don't have as many races listed there. The Association of International Marathons and Distance Races, one of the governing bodies of the sport, has a pretty good calendar too.

To find events in Africa, South America, or Oceania, however, one must be a little more resourceful. You can't just Google "marathons in Africa," even if a smattering of races does pop up. There are actually plenty of races, especially in South Africa where running is a popular sport. The problem is figuring out how to register for them, since the dates always seem to be a moving target. Fortunately, there are marathon "hobbyists" who build websites with titles like "Jeremy's Eclectic Marathon Page." They are a good starting place for obscure marathons that don't seem to make the mainstream calendars.

After hours of scouring the Internet, I settled on a path that would start in mid-February in Birmingham, Alabama, and lead me to Luxor, Egypt; Valencia, Spain; King George Island, Antarctica; Ushuaia, Argentina; Jenolan Caves west of Sydney, Australia; and, finally, to Seoul, South Korea.

Finally, a schedule that allowed me to finish in 35 days was in place. After several months of jockeying the schedule around, I thought I had come up with something that would put me in the record book and keep me there for quite a while.

Time would tell.

There was a little competition out there too. In December 2006, Tim Harris of England started his own quest that would lower the bar to about 45 days, ending on January 29th, 2007. It was great to know he would establish a new record before me, so he could enjoy the record for a short time before it was broken, since my attempt wouldn't start until after he finished. Tim's African marathon was cancelled, though, but he found another one and broke the world record in about 91 days. Although 45 days would have taken a lot of time off the record, 35 days seemed like a record that would be pretty tough to beat.

Thinking maybe this was my chance at stardom, I sent out press releases before I began my adventure. The public knowledge that the record was being challenged found its way into the Marathon Tours newsletter late in 2006. By the time I boarded the ship to Antarctica, international marathoners joining me on that trip would know of the quest.

On February 9, 2007, my adventure to the ends of the earth began by boarding a plane for Birmingham, Alabama, for the Mercedes Marathon. While marathons were the trip's central component, they were also the conduits to adventure. Along the way, I hoped to climb a couple mountains, make new friends, and sample tasty beers on every continent.

North America: Mercedes Benz Marathon, Birmingham, Alabama

A day before the marathon, I took an hour-and-a-half drive to Cheaha Mountain to check off another state high point from my list; at 2,413 feet, the mountain is the highest point in Alabama. In 2003, as I approached the end of my circuit of running a marathon in each of the 50 states, I learned of the Highpointers Club, which I promptly joined.

Their goal is to visit the highest point in each of the 50 states. Cheaha was an easy "drive up" mountain, but as long as I was in the neighborhood, it seemed like the thing to do.

That night, in response to a press release, a reporter and a cameraman from a local station came to interview me and to film me running for a few minutes. *The Birmingham News* reporter Solomon Crenshaw interviewed me as well, so before starting, the local crowd had at least a piece of what was going on.

The Mercedes Marathon in Birmingham began on a beautiful, sunny Sunday morning, and at the starting gun, the world-record clock started ticking away the minutes, hours, and days to my goal. Before the 2-mile mark, I came upon four women from back home in Grand Rapids. We ran together for a bit before I went on ahead. I had started pretty much in the back of the pack, so I enjoyed gradually passing runners and even an occasional pace group.

Around mile 18 came the first evidence that my publicity machine was working well. We ran through a residential neighborhood, and in front of the Larussa home were a couple signs in the front yard. One read "Go Kern Go!" and the other was a drawing of the seven continents. I stopped to say hello and thank them for the encouragement. One of the Larussa kids gave me an American flag bandana; I tied it around my neck and posed with him for a quick picture. I wore it to the finish line, and it became my good luck charm in each subsequent marathon. I don't know if the Larussas kept up with my adventure after that. I hope so.

The course feature that stands out most in my mind was a long hill that spanned nearly 2 miles starting at around mile 21. After the long climb, the course flattened out for the remainder of the run. The first leg of the adventure ended in 4 hours, 30 minutes, and 39 seconds (4:30:39).

One marathon down, six to go. Come, Watson, come! The game is afoot.

Africa: The Egyptian International Marathon, Luxor, Egypt

After a quick trip home interrupted by an overnight stop in Chicago—thank you, United Airlines—I left Tuesday afternoon for the trip to Luxor for the Egyptian International Marathon on Friday, February 16. After spending a day in Amsterdam, which included a tour of the Anne Frank House, I boarded another overnight flight with a stopover in Cairo before it went on to Luxor.

As I left the terminal after landing, trying to figure out how to get to the hotel, about 20 taxi drivers accosted me. They all wanted to take me, but none would quote me a price. They wanted me to tell them how much. I started walking to a car with one driver, but before I knew it, another approached and the two of them started a heated argument. I turned and walked away, but they followed me, and more joined the fray. Finally, the committee must have agreed because they picked a winner amongst themselves. Later, I found out I paid about twice what I should have, but after the thirty-minute drive, I was happy to pay the 15 Euros and be done with the madness.

The marathon was a big event in Luxor, with much of the city turning out the day before the event for a ceremonial run through the town. I arrived just in time to change into running clothes before joining the "parade" for a two-kilometer run through the downtown area. Actually, it was more of a walk, with the local dignitaries making appearances, and families, ox carts, bicycles, and even a couple motorized vehicles joining in the fun.

The next morning after an early breakfast and a forty-five minute bus ride to the starting line, the marathon started. Spectators included scores of goats, sheep, and donkeys, along with plenty of people going about their daily lives. Most of them, both livestock and people, looked up occasionally, with only mild curiosity. After running out about a kilometer, we began the first of four 10K loops. Most of the route went around an array of farms with sugar cane, clover, and other crops dotting the landscape. Locals piled clover onto donkey-drawn carts to feed their animals; other carts were loaded with sugar cane.

Toward the end of the loop, two older men sat beside the road keeping an eye on a pile of onions. Each time we passed, the pile grew larger, and by the time I reached the fourth loop, the pile was enormous. The younger people still came to the pile with armloads of freshly harvested onions. Life in the area seemed simple, and everyone along the way was nice. Children would join us at different points along the course saying things like "Welcome to Egypt" and "What's your nationality?" With temperatures reaching the low 80s, the heat started to take its toll, but I still managed to cross the finish line in 4:47:06.

Europe: Maratón Popular de Valencia, Valencia, Spain

Two marathons were complete, but I had less than forty-eight hours to get to Valencia, Spain, for the Maratón Popular de Valencia. After leaving the hotel in Luxor at about 5 a.m. on Saturday, I'd spend the next night in Valencia, Spain.

One guy I didn't meet when I ran in Egypt was Richard Takata, a Toronto native who had completed his first marathon in 1996. At that time, he was an overweight smoker who could barely walk up a flight of stairs without gasping for air. Over the years, though, he lost more than 50 pounds and ran more than 50 marathons while raising money for a variety of charities. He was also running in Valencia. Pictures from my camera would later reveal that we ran nearly side-by-side in Luxor, but we didn't meet there. Nor did we meet in Spain. That pleasure would come a few days later.

For some strange reason, I had no soreness in my legs when I started the third leg of my journey, the Maratón Popular de Valencia, on February 18. The route was mostly city streets, and I fell in with a group of runners from Great Britain for a while, welcoming the English language conversation. That's one of the things we take for granted, I suppose, but in a country where the dominant language is Spanish (it's

Spain, after all), there is a limited numbers of people with whom to talk. "Animo!" is the common cheer from the sidelines, which translates to "I animate" technically but is more like "look alive, go for it" in this context. I made sure to listen.

It was a nice day, and I finished the first 20 kilometers in two hours. I had a pretty good idea by then that it would be my fastest of the first three continents, and that proved true. It was my third marathon in eight days, so the faster finish at 4:27:26 boosted my attitude substantially. Three up, three down, with a rest week coming before the Antarctica Marathon on February 26.

Antarctica: The Last Marathon, King George Island off the Antarctica Peninsula

The first time I met Richard Takata, or so I thought, was in Buenos Aires en route to the Antarctica Marathon. He was wearing a shirt from the Maratón Popular de Valencia. The 185 of us who would run in Antarctica gathered for a reception before flying to Ushuaia, the world's southernmost city, where we would board two Russian research ships. The *Akademik Vavilov* and the *Akademik Ioffe* would serve as our home for over a week as we crossed the Drake Passage to Antarctica. Richard and I were shipmates on the *Ioffe* (pronounced like coffee, but with a Y instead of a C at the beginning).

"You're the talk of the ship," Richard said to me. Because of the pre-marathon information sent out by Marathon Tours prior to the trip, everyone on the ship knew of my attempt at the record book. Richard was also running the continents in a short period of time. We weren't best buddies or anything, but we sometimes ate at the same table on the ship and had a conversation or two along the way. During the Antarctica Marathon, we took pictures of each other on the course.

After a two-day crossing of the Drake Passage, we arrived at King George Island for the Antarctica Marathon. The temperatures weren't too cold, hovering only around the freezing mark. It was the wind and the sideways snow that would really make it an adventure. We started at the Russian research base, Bellingshausen, and headed through a mud field toward Collins Glacier. Thanks to a dusting of fresh snow and the cool temperatures, the mud wasn't bad on the first lap. The course took us to the base of the glacier, then went straight up it for a five-kilometer out-and-back. We then headed back to Bellingshausen, then out the other direction through the Chilean base to the Great Wall of China, a Chinese base, then to the finish line.

The second time heading out through the mud field, the feet of 185 runners had churned the mud into a gooey, shoe-sucking mush. Curling my toes to keep my shoes on, I kept my shoes firmly on my feet. For some reason, Collins Glacier seemed a lot longer on the second climb. One more time back through the mud, past the finish, and out to the Great Wall and back, and I completed marathon number four in a time of 6:16:52.

Two different women broke the women's record for running all seven continents that day. Jeanne Stawiecki finished the seven continents in 141 days as she crossed the finish line on February 26th. A couple hours later, her world record was broken by Ginny Turner, who lowered the women's mark to 113 days.

The Antarctica Marathon, known as "The Last Marathon," was conceived by Thom Gilligan of Marathon Tours and Travel, and was first run in 1995. The marathon is the reason most of us signed up, but the adventure became the main point of the trip. After finishing the marathon, there were still a few days where we would experience the majesty of Antarctica.

Marathon Tours also organized the "Antarctic Kayak Championships." Finals would pit those of us on the *Ioffe* against our colleagues on the *Vavilov*. As we prepared for our qualifying race to select our team, we rafted together among the ice flows in a quiet sound. As we waited for the crew to move far enough away to set up a finish line for us, a pair of humpback whales came fairly close to us, breaching the surface and lazing around in the water as we stared. Ice floes, whales, glacier-covered mountains in the distance, and the cleanest air on the planet. Magic.

As the race started, I was surprised to be one of the fastest of the bunch. Only Bruce Austin, a runner from Corvalis, Oregon, beat me to the finish line, so along with two more of our shipmates, we would represent the *Ioffe* in the finals. Yeah, Bruce and I were the studs on our ship, but a couple days later, our friends from the *Vavilov* crushed us.

We spent the rest of the trip traveling up and down the Antarctic Peninsula, stopping at penguin rookeries, cruising around icy bays where we would look for seals lying around on small icebergs, and seeing an occasional whale. Penguins, primarily Adelies, Chinstraps, and Gentoos, were nearly everywhere we landed. The rules said stay 25 yards away from them. They didn't know the rules, however, and came close enough to occasionally poop all over our boots.

On a small island where no animals lived, we had the experience of camping out for one night, giving many in the group their first opportunity to camp in Antarctica. There were no campfires, and really all we did was land, hang out for a while, and sack out. In the morning, just after the Zodiacs arrived to pick us up to return us to the ship, a loud crack across the bay alerted us to look up just in time to see an iceberg calving off a glacier. It crashed into the water, sending a miniature tsunami right at us. As it reached the Zodiacs, it flipped one over. Fortunately we weren't on our way back to the ship yet.

In the history of Earth, the number of visitors to Antarctica would populate only a very small city. It was my third time to experience the White Continent, and again, bonds of friendship were created that will last a lifetime.

South America: Fin del Mundo, Ushuaia, Argentina

Our ships enjoyed a smooth trip back across the Drake to Ushuaia for the March 6 Fin del Mundo (End of the World) Marathon. I had come down with a cold on the trip from Antarctica, which would make the run a little more difficult. We started our South America marathon at Tierra del Fuego National Park at the south end of Route 3 (which begins in Alaska and runs all the way through North and South America). The route took us up some rolling hills and through a forest. Around the 12-mile mark, we turned right along the bay toward the airport for a 5K out-and-back run section. The wind coming off the water was so stiff it actually interfered with the swing of my legs, causing me to kick my ankle as my foot swung past it several times. Bruce Austin was on his way back and we met each other at the aid station.

"It's the first time I've ever had water blow out of my cup," he said.

It was one of those winds that never seemed to be at your back, even with multiple bends of the road as we ran to the airport and back. I was really relieved to have that part of the course behind me. After slogging through the final remaining 11 miles, I crossed the finish line in 5:24:37.

That afternoon, a few of us, including Richard Takata and I, got together for lunch in Ushuaia to celebrate our accomplishment. I would head off to Australia the next day. Richard was headed for Cypress. I wondered what his time frame was and what the rest of the journey would bring.

Two more marathons were left on my itinerary.

Oceania: The Six Foot Track Marathon, Katoomba to Jenolan Caves, NSW, Australia

My good friends Brent Weigner and Paul Ruesch joined me for the final two legs of the trip, meeting me at the airport in Sydney. The Six Foot Track Marathon in Australia was held on March 10, and I expected it to be the toughest of the seven races. I was right. The course consisted of a series of trails starting in Katoomba, New South Wales, about three hours west of Sydney, and ending at Jenolan Caves, a distance of 45 kilometers. That's nearly 3K longer than a normal marathon, and the course had a strict seven-hour cutoff. Brent, Paul, and I showed up to pick up our race packets the day before the race.

"It was going to be a tough trail race with some big ups and downs," Brent recalled. "We would have to wade across a river. The weather was expected to be very hot. We had to qualify for the race to begin with as it is one of the premier races in Australia—and the three of us didn't exactly look like seasoned marathon runners after dragging ourselves halfway around the world to get there."

Brent remembers Kevin Tiller, the race director, wearing a doubtful look as we picked up our numbers the day before. He wished us luck, then added, "You will need it."

Thanks, buddy.

At the end of every wave of runners was "The Sweeper," an experienced trail runner, running with a broom that signified you better darn well stay ahead of him or you wouldn't get an official finish. I was nervous.

"I remember drawing race bib number 666 and then meeting a guy dressed as the Grim Reaper at the start," Paul said. "Thinking this was bad luck, Don suggested I turn the number upside down to make it number 999 which I did and then walked right into some lady who had the legitimate number 999 bib so we had a good laugh, took a picture and then I had to put my number back."

The course started on a narrow path downhill over wet rocks for about twenty-five minutes, and Brent, Paul, and I carefully worked our way down to avoid slipping on the wet rocks. The path became wide enough to run side by side as we progressed through the beautiful open land. We learned about bell birds as we ran through one forested area and heard them "ringing" all around us. After a while, we started down a fairly steep path that took us down to a small stream. We waded across it and continued over a knoll where we would find the *real* stream—a small river with a rope strung across it to keep us from being swept downstream by the swiftly flowing water.

| and the adventure continues....

The water was over our waists, and there was no other way but through it. On the other side, we stopped to dump the gravel out of our socks. Then we started up two half-hour or better slogs uphill. As we finished the second climb, we came into an aid station and found a sign that said 19K to go. As we replenished with some food and drink, and Paul sat down to shake gravel out of his socks, the man with the broom crested the hill behind us.

We were caught by The Grim Sweeper.

"I hope you're ahead of schedule," I said.

"Actually, I'm about a minute behind."

"Crap." (Perhaps not my actual word.) He left the aid station ahead of us. Paul looked up and saw the expression on my face. "Just go! I'll catch up!" I chased down The Sweeper listening to him warn runners he passed of the need to finish ahead of him or not get a medal. I squeaked past him and picked up a very small lead.

He came into the aid station behind me, but I left while he was still drinking and eating. Still, I could hear his warnings behind me. It got under my skin just a little bit, but it motivated me to get me the heck away from the guy with the broom. My pace quickened enough so his warnings faded out of earshot. The man with the broom faded into the past, never to be seen or heard for the rest of the trail. At least by me.

The day before I left on the trip, I had talked to my dad. "Do you really think you can run all those marathons?" he had asked in a tone that left me feeling like he doubted my abilities. It was the perfect example of something I've come to call "Motivation by Aggravation." As I worked up and down the hills of the last 15 kilometers, those words came into my head again. "Well, stand back and watch this, Dad!" I didn't come all this way to screw it up at marathon number six.

I caught up with Brent with about six kilometers to go—he had been suffering from the heat. "I ran out of electrolytes, and some guy helped me out with salt tablets," he told me as we ran through the final kilometers.

Soon, a full marathon distance was complete, but due to the length of the trail, this one was 45K long. The final three kilometers went steeply downhill. My strides were short and my quads burned as I ran down the gravel path toward the finish. Finally, a piece of paved trail with a handrail signaled the entrance to Jenolan Caves Park. In the distance, the announcer called Brent's name as he finished. *Stay vertical for a couple more minutes!* Then it was the announcer's turn to call my name. My official time was 6:45:03. My legs screamed and I desperately needed a beer, but it was the most satisfying finish of my life. Only a few minutes later, Paul handily beat the sweeper to the finish line.

We managed to find a beer on the way back to our room, but as we finished showering and laid around for just a minute, we were *gone*. Somewhere around 9 p.m., our growling stomachs woke us. We were starving. After the much needed rest, we now needed some serious nutrition. Unfortunately, the kitchen was done cooking for the night. Taking stock of our meager supply of power bars, the silver-tongued Paul said, "Just a minute," and walked through the swinging staff-only door into the kitchen. He emerged a couple minutes later, soon followed by three plates of huge hamburgers and piles of fries. The cook was apparently convinced that letting foreigners starve in his establishment wasn't the best idea. I don't recall a more satisfying hamburger than the one I ate that night.

The next day, we headed south for the Snowy Mountains. After all, we had a few days, so climbing Mount Kosciuszko, the highest point in Australia, seemed like a good idea. As we made our way through Australia, Paul remembered that Marcus Fillinger, a friend we met while the three of us were at the North Pole Marathon in 2003, lived somewhere on this side of the country. Paul keeps a good bit of data in his Palm Pilot, and he happened to have Marcus' number. As it turned out, Marcus has a ranch on the road between where we were and the Snowy Mountains. We made out for his Alpha Dog Ranch and spent the early part of the evening drinking beers with Marcus and his girlfriend

Shannon before heading farther south.

The next morning, Paul, Brent, and I took the ski lift from Thredbo Ski Resort up to the highest pub in Australia, which is also the trailhead for the climb up to Australia's highest point, Mount Kosciuszko. Some consider Kosciuszko one of the seven summits (highest point on each continent). Most serious climbers go with Oceania or Australasia as the continent, and thus figure Carstensz Pyramid in Indonesia as the high point. But, well, we weren't in Indonesia. Nor could we be considered serious climbers.

The climb should have been an easy one. Where the trail wasn't well-groomed gravel, it was metal grating over sensitive areas, creating an elevated surface to protect delicate plant life. On our six legs that Australia's toughest marathon had just beaten up, it wasn't quite as easy of a hike as we may have liked. After only an hour or so of hiking, though, we arrived at the highest point in Australia, 7,310 feet above sea level.

"My feet were blistered up pretty good from that whole water/sand in the shoes bit from the race," Paul said. "So I bought some Crocs at a shop near the base, and the only color they had in my size was purple. I was amazed at how many people take notice of other people's shoes, as I got a lot of weird looks from there on out. I went up in those sandals and still have them to this day, still get a lot of weird looks too, though my wife says it's not only the shoes." (Notice that where Paul says "people take notice," he more accurately should have said everyone was giving him sh*t.)

We spent that evening at Thredbo before heading out the next day to explore more of Australia. On the way back to Sydney, we stopped to see Marcus again for an evening of beers and meat on the "barbie." As Marcus threw steaks, brats, burgers, and other assorted pieces of meat onto the grill, I looked at him and asked how many people he was expecting. "Oh, it's just us." Sure enough, before the night was over, Paul, Brent, Marcus, his girlfriend Shannon, and I had polished off enough meat to feed a small third-world country.

South Korea: Donga Marathon, Seoul

The final leg of the seven continents trip was the March 18 Donga Marathon in Seoul, which would prove the easiest of the seven marathons.

At Inchon airport, about a half-hour outside of Seoul, three Americans tried to make sense of the signs and debated how to get into Seoul. Paul said something then that sticks with me to this day: "I say we just throw ourselves into the public transportation system and see what happens." Hey, two of the best guys in the world were there to keep me out of trouble. We walked out of the airport and found a bus that seemed to be the airport shuttle to downtown Seoul.

South Koreans have no street numbers on their buildings. The cities are organized by areas in a way I can't explain, but somehow we figured out how to get where we were going with a minimal amount of trouble. The regular bus stop was only a block or two from our hotel.

We also had the advantage of having a tour guide once we got there. Paul's cousin Matt and his girlfriend Su-Jin met us later that day, and they helped us find our way around. We made our way to the marathon headquarters and found the special area for international runners to pick up our race numbers.

We had a couple days to play before the marathon, so we spent a good deal of time in the various street markets. On the streets of Seoul, bootleg DVDs of movies are available quite freely for only a little bit of cash, so we picked up some cheap entertainment.

The next day, we visited a several-block-long marketplace, buying souvenirs and enjoying the culture. It was March 17, the day before race day. Brent was feeling the need to relax before race day and left Paul and me to our own devices as he headed back to the hotel for some down time.

At least that's how I remembered it.

"I had booked our hotel at the recommendation of my cousin Matt who lives in Daegu," Paul said. "He came up, and we hung out with him and his girlfriend Su-Jin. They took us to a market where a lot of shady dealing goes on and said to play it cool down this one stretch of vendors. I look back and see Don in full negotiations with this shady guy trying to sell him pirated movies on DVD, and my cousin helplessly trying to get him out of there and translate and keep him from getting knifed. I decided I could not watch and checked back about ten minutes later to see that they'd all made best friends and were talking like long lost buddies."

What can I say? I'm a people person.

Meanwhile, the carts of cardboard that kept heading down one of the side streets intrigued Paul, who happens to work for the EPA. We followed them and found their destination at the end of the street, where the carts were unloaded and the cardboard baled to be sent off for recycling. Paul made friends with a fairly ancient man who spoke almost no English but was very happy to have new friends. He managed to find out how old we were at least, and then pulled out a few small paper cups and a bottle of soju, Korea's national liquor, and poured us each a cup. A full cup. We toasted our new friendship, and he handed us a pair of chopsticks, pointing to something on a plate that I'm sure had good things in it but nothing I recognized.

Well, actually, the contents of the plate reminded us of puke. We each tried a bit and discovered the taste was much better than the appearance. Another cup of soju to wash it down, and the three of us were starting to feel quite happy. Apparently, drinking on the job isn't a problem. Or perhaps our host was the boss, making up his own rules. We bid our new friend farewell and found a place to get a meal to absorb some of the warm feelings in our stomachs.

That night was St. Patrick's Day, and as it happens, there was an Irish Pub only a block from our hotel. It was only logical to enjoy our pre-race dinner there. Pints of Guinness and plates of sushi are not the usual pre-race meal but proved very satisfying, nonetheless. Signs in the windows announced the holiday, but apparently no one received the memo, so the "party" for St. Paddy's was just Paul and me and a table of eight South Koreans oblivious to the occasion.

Race day was pretty uneventful, except for the culture shock of walking into a Port-a-Potty and realizing that to relieve oneself, one must climb up on a platform, put feet on the designated spots, and squat over a hole in the platform. If nothing else, Koreans have totally solved the problem of cold toilet seats.

Compared to the previous week's adventure, we had an easy day. The weather was perfect—sunny and somewhere in the high 40s or low 50s—the course was flat, and the kids along the course were a kick. Groups of kids would hold out their hands for high fives from the three Americans and then go crazy, giggling as we ran on. We were three amigos, sticking together for the whole marathon, running dead-even splits between the first and second half. As our friends back home were still in the midst of their St. Patrick's Day celebrations, we ran into the Olympic Stadium, finishing with a lap around the track where a few years earlier many records had been set or broken. We crossed the finish line in 4:35:30, completing the mission, breaking the world record in 34 days, 13 hours, and 43 minutes.

Maybe.

The amigos spent a while celebrating, then worked our way through the subway system back to our hotel for a final dinner together. The next morning, I dragged my gear to the shuttle bus stop for the final leg of the journey. Home.

A day later and half a world away, the lovely Francine had organized a "hero's welcome" at Gerald R. Ford International Airport in Grand Rapids. Friends were there wearing special "I Conquered the World" shirts she had made for the occasion, and my granddaughters were there, excited to see Grandpa. The Grand Rapids Press sent a reporter for an interview. We all headed to Schmohz Brewery for a bit of celebration.

Sharing the moment with friends and family is always the best part of a journey. It's not the summit of the mountain that counts; it's returning to base camp. I had returned to base camp. Time to celebrate.

A couple days later while looking over photos and writing some journal entries, I made some discoveries. First, there was that very nice picture of Richard Takata from the Egyptian Marathon on my camera. I wondered what he really had done. A quick Internet search confirmed it.

Richard had set the mark at 29 days, 16 hours, and 17 minutes in Ushuaia, Argentina, when I still had two more races to complete. And while I had strong suspicions, I hadn't realized that as we ate lunch celebrating our marathon finish in Ushuaia, we were also celebrating Richard's new world record, taking more than 60 days off the previous mark.

For the next five minutes, I was busy sorting out my emotional state and feeling a little disappointed. There were lots of things to feel, but never did anger, depression, or regret creep in to the mix. Why should they? The goal was met. The previous record was blown out of the water, I was currently in second place in the world record rankings, and one of the few (you could count them on one fairly deformed hand at the time) who had run all seven continents twice. The adventure was epic, a "trip of a lifetime," filled with new friends and experiences.

From Feb. 9 to March 20, I had slept six nights on airplanes and eight nights aboard a ship. I was in the air for more than 40,000 miles and spent countless hours riding around in buses, taxis, and other forms of public transportation. I nailed every goal I had set. Except one. The record book would now read:

MARATHON ON EACH CONTINENT - MEN

The shortest overall time to complete a marathon on each of the seven continents is 29 days, 16 hours, and 17 minutes by Richard Takata (Canada) from 4 February - 6 March 2007.

For now.

Chapter 5

The Nemesis?

If I had owned the world record for even a minute, that would have been the end of the story. Guinness would have recognized the mark and given me a certificate, and for the rest of my life, I could claim I had a Guinness World Record. Mission accomplished.

There was only one problem: Richard Takata.

While I was busy doing press releases about my upcoming record, Richard was planning his own attempt. The information made it into Marathon Tours' newsletter, and when Richard saw it, he did what anyone else would do. He rearranged his schedule to do what he set out to do—get the world record.

After running with Richard in four consecutive marathons, it started to become clear that publicizing the attempt in advance was less than wise. While the world was keeping up with my plan, Richard was flying under the radar. One of the things I like about him is he always was the gentleman, never wanting to spoil my trip by telling me of his success, knowing I had two more legs to run.

Suspicions of his intent also kept me from questioning him too thoroughly. There was no sense spoiling a great trip with my own curiosity. It just didn't seem like the thing to do. The only thing I didn't like is he was more popular with women on the ship than I was. Whose fault was that?

The reactions among my friends were more dramatic, for the most part. Many followed me and posted comments as the adventure progressed. Nasreen Fynewever, a teacher here in my hometown of Grand Rapids, had shared and followed the journey with her class. They became some of my biggest fans. Here's my interaction with her class in response to the "disappointment" when I shared the news that Takata had broken the world record:

Nasreen: "My classes really feel for you. Tons read about you yesterday in the paper. Any chance that other guy ran a bad marathon?"

Me: "No, he's legit. Just did what he had to do. I appreciate the way they feel for me too, but I'm really just fine. What record I'm going for next? Maybe the longest chain of paper clips. Or maybe I'll start growing my fingernails. I'm sure I'll come up with something at some point, but probably not today. Let your kids know that sometimes we get disappointed, but it's really about the attitude. I've had an AMAZING journey, inspired hundreds of people, made a positive impact on people I love, and met tons of new friends.

So, Richard got the record. Things like that happen. I'm cool. Well, mostly."

Nasreen: "I relayed your thanks for the message to my students already, but I actually ended up reading it to them. They thought you were very cool and collected. You truly do inspire, even in these moments where the recent adventure needs to be put in perspective. I don't think I have admired you more than I did during a moment in the sixth hour when the students were saying things like 'Wow, he has a really cool attitude' and 'That is even cooler than all the races.' My heart just felt proud to know you."

Richard's true role was that of a catalyst. He gave me a chance to again inspire some pretty neat young people. He taught me that a guy can run a marathon on Saturday west of the International Date Line and on Sunday east of it because of the time change. But most importantly, he gave me a chance to do the whole thing one more time. At least.

So following the five minutes spent sorting out my emotional state after learning of Richard's record, the inevitable question popped into my consciousness: *I wonder what the schedule looks like around the Antarctic Ice Marathon in December?*

Disappointment suddenly gave way to planning.

In 2002, Adventure Network International (ANI), a travel company specializing in expeditions to Antarctica, organized a marathon at the Geographic South Pole. The trip was a fiasco, ending in controversy, a lawsuit, and ultimately a change in ANI ownership. Irishman Richard Donovan won that event, the only South Pole Marathon ever held. Later that winter, he flew to the North Pole to run 26.2 miles there as well, becoming the first to cover the marathon distance at both geographic poles.

A natural organizer, Donovan quickly put together two of the most extreme marathons on earth: The North Pole Marathon, and the Antarctic Ice Marathon. I was very familiar with Richard's race in Antarctica because in 2002, we shared that South Pole experience, and then in 2003, I ran in his first North Pole Marathon. It was time to get reacquainted with my old friend.

On December 12, 2007, the third running of the Antarctic Ice Marathon was scheduled. If it was possible to schedule around that event, the world record might be obtainable even during the same year. The gears in my brain were probably making enough noise to disturb those around me as a new plan was devised. Within a few days, a tentative schedule was taking form.

My next run for the record book would begin the Sunday before Thanksgiving.

In February and March of 2007, I learned a great deal that would boost my confidence level. I was capable of running marathons close together. Sleeping on airplanes was a skill developed by years of practice. Solutions for jet lag (get up and run a marathon the next morning), odd meal schedules (eat when you feel like it), foreign languages (all you really need to know is how to find a beer and a bathroom), and other problems come naturally. Call it confident ignorance or informed insanity, but in a very short time, it was clear that breaking the record yet again during 2007 was within my grasp.

Richard Takata was never my nemesis. He was my inspiration. He would have the world record for a while. But he motivated me to look for better ways. He had moved the mark from 91 days down to under 30, though. The next attempt wouldn't be so easy.

More Competition?

Sticking with a goal is the key to success, and no one I encountered in my travels sets that example better than Dr. William Tan. In 2005, William attempted to set the world record for completing all seven continents in the shortest period of time. He fell short in the Antarctica Marathon, unable to finish the course before it was time to return to the ship. In February 2007, he was also on the trip to Antarctica. While he made another valiant attempt, he again failed to finish the course due to the time constraints on King George Island. William wasn't a rival for the record, however. He was in a different division. He had to deal with numerous extra details. You see, Dr. Tan races in a wheelchair.

From his website: "Dr. William Tan personifies both passion and compassion. He contracted polio at the age of two and is paralyzed from the waist down. Notwithstanding his disability, he has shown outstanding strength in overcoming adversities."

There's a lot more, but to summarize, William is a neuroscientist, physician, and Paralympian. He's super-educated, cares about people, and has more degrees than a thermometer. I was impressed by his soft-spoken answers as we appeared on Argentine television together. They were interviewing a few participants in their race who had also done the Antarctica Marathon.

Our first conversation took place in an elevator a few minutes after the broadcast. In spite of failing to finish in Antarctica for the second time in two attempts, he wasn't ready to stop. His great attitude and determination inspired me. The connection between us was immediate, and common purposes created an instant friendship. In spite of missing his mark for the second time, it was clear that giving up wasn't part of his nature. Someday, he would get the record he sought. The next day, we both finished the marathon in Ushuaia.

The records we sought were different. Like other marathon records, the wheelchair division is a separate category. His 2007 attempt may have been unsuccessful, but by this time, you know my record attempt didn't work out as planned either. Having that in common created a special bond between us. Though it was unspoken, when we parted, one thing was certain. We'd see each other again.

It wouldn't be very long.

Chapter 6

Around the World (Again)

Running marathons is a great hobby, but in the years since 2004, *running* a marathon was well on the way to being my main occupation. So before I could go off on another big adventure, I needed to work for a few months.

When Millennium Park opened in Grand Rapids in early 2004, it provided what looked like an ideal venue for a new event. Being natural instigators, one of my best friends Shawn Sweet and I started the Grand Rapids Marathon. The event moved to downtown Grand Rapids in 2005, and in 2007, Metro Health Hospital became our title sponsor. I spent much of the time between my two record attempts organizing the event.

In early October 2007, as we prepared for our fourth running, an unexpected act of nature moved me along the road to being a full-time race director.

The Chicago Marathon, held on October 7, made history as one of the hottest fall weekends on record. The heat caused the cancellation of the race after it started. While I went on to finish the race, many runners followed the instructions of race officials to get onto buses or take the shorter path back to the finish. Thus, they were denied completing the goal they had worked for all summer. Many of the more than 30,000 runners wilted into a mass of hot, sweaty humanity.

As a pace group leader, I led a group of runners attempting to finish the 26.2-mile distance in a time of five hours and fifteen minutes. By 16 miles, we had passed through three different aid stations that were totally out of water. By the time we reached 19 miles, the police and course volunteers were herding people onto a bus or instructing them to walk via the most direct route back to the starting area near Grant Park.

Two women running with my pace group stuck with me, and together we finished the course, finding drinks and ways to cool off anywhere we could. A few fire hydrants had been opened along the course, and we found two Cokes and three bottles of water on a curb beside a woman who told us to help ourselves. Dropping out of a marathon never seemed acceptable to me.

A desperately miserable day was made more bearable, however, knowing that the runners who couldn't finish would soon seek a way to put the summer's training to good use. Three weeks later on October 28, the Grand Rapids Marathon was scheduled. My marathon. The drive home from Chicago was filled with anticipation, suspecting what would be confirmed upon arriving at home with a quick check of email. An inbox full of registrations greeted me. Runners who had been kicked off the Chicago course found a way to use that training, and we were it.

We scrambled to order more medals and shirts and bumped up our food orders. By race weekend, our numbers were up from 1,700 runners in 2006 to over 2,800. We were on the map in a big way. Our October ended with a bang, and the word-of-mouth advertising we receive from our friends in Chicago continues to this day because of the great

Chicago Marathon Meltdown.

It was our most successful event to date, both in terms of numbers and in execution. With my biggest workload of the year behind me, it was time for another attempt at the world record. This time would be even more intense. Richard Takata had moved the old record down to less than a month. It wasn't as breakable as it had been before.

On November 15, 2007, I found myself once again sitting at Gerald R. Ford International Airport in Grand Rapids, excited for yet another global adventure. On a continual high after a successful Grand Rapids Marathon and running all seven continents in only 35 days, I was off for another try. This time, it was scheduled for only 25 days. I confidently expected the world record would fall this time.

Marathon Tours' Antarctica Marathon, known as "The Last Marathon" on King George Island, was reached by ship from Ushuaia, Argentina. The Antarctic Ice Marathon was scheduled to run on December 12 at a camp in the Patriot Hills in the Ellsworth Mountains. A plane trip to the interior of the continent from Punta Arenas, Chile, was the only way there.

Was it possible to work around the Ice Marathon and schedule marathons in less than 30 days? Searching the Internet, emailing South Africa and New Zealand, and figuring out finances to put another plan together made for a challenging summer, but the plan solidified with plenty of time to spare. Round two would start in Beirut, Lebanon, on the Sunday before Thanksgiving. Atlanta, Georgia, held a marathon on Thanksgiving Day, a convenient mid-week marathon. Florence, Italy; Port Elizabeth, South Africa; Wanganui, New Zealand; Viña del Mar, Chile; and, finally, the Antarctic Ice Marathon would complete the trip. The schedule seemed to work. I was feeling confident that this time, if everything went according to plan, it would soon be my name in the record book.

Asia: Beirut, Lebanon—November 18, 2007

By early morning on November 16, I was in Frankfurt, Germany, en route to my first marathon in Beirut, Lebanon. I arrived in the Middle East at the airport in Beirut. Lebanon had no visa requirements for Americans, so customs was a breeze. The only thing they check is whether there is a stamp from Israel in your passport. Fortunately, my passport was new since my 1998 trip to Israel, so there were no complications.

The adventure was under way, and once again negotiating taxi fare in an unfamiliar country provided a fine way to part company with a few more dollars than necessary. Taxi drivers make sport of deciding who will be the lucky driver to get the fare, but after a bit of haggling, I was on my way to downtown Beirut.

Drivers in Lebanon are some of the most alert people in the world. They have no choice. The lane lines, the stop lights, and any other indicator of where traffic should go are treated as mere suggestions. It seemed the driver knew exactly where his car left off and the next car started, and somehow managed to keep just enough distance between them to slip a piece of paper or two. We finally figured out where my hotel was, and after talking to a couple people there, I learned once again that the correct price for the taxi was about half what my new friends charged me.

Beirut is really a beautiful city, and if the political unrest ever gets resolved, it would be an even better vacation destination. In spite of obvious bullet damage to many of the buildings, and despite much of the downtown area being barricaded, it was a busy, cosmopolitan city. Armed guards on nearly every corner kept things safe, so there was no worry when walking around the streets.

At race number pickup at the ABC Mall, a kid at the registration desk gave me the phone number of Mark Dickinson, the race director, who invited me to have lunch with him, the elite runners, and various other international attendees. He was excited to have his race be the first in my journey. The next discovery was amusing.

The Beirut Marathon was touted as an event of more than 18,000 runners. That part was true. However, out of those 18,000, only 340 were set to compete in the marathon. Around 13,800 had registered for the 10K event, and another 5,200 in the 5K. On the official registration closing date, only 1,000 of the 18,000 were registered. I'm glad I didn't have to order T-shirts for this event.

Combining the jetlag and a midday nap, sleep that night was evasive. Any kind of rest is good, however, so I lay relaxing in bed before nodding off sometime after 1 a.m. Between 2 and 3 a.m., my buddy Paul Ruesch called.

"Hey man, it's the middle of the night," I said.

"Dude, where are you?"

"I'm in Beirut."

"Oh, this phone call must be costing you a fortune," Paul said. "I got your Antarctica stuff. Look forward to seeing you in South America." Paul would join me in Chile for the marathon there. I had dropped a big bag of Antarctic gear on his porch in Chicago before embarking on the trip.

Two hours later, the alarm went off. As I left to head over to the Radisson to catch the marathon shuttle, a small bus with four runners pulled up and stopped. They were looking for directions to the hotel. Fortunately, I knew where I was going.

They quickly offered, "Come ride with us."

They gave me a ride in exchange for the proper guidance. Good thing, too, because the bus driver was going to turn right when he should have turned left.

I'm not sure where I first met Andy Kotulski, but I recognized him from the marathon circuit. He was in Beirut to celebrate his sixty-eighth birthday by running his 590th marathon. We all boarded the buses, and while I talked to a young couple behind me, someone lifted my cap to see who I was.

"I thought that was you!" Scott McIvor said.

Scott is a stud athlete, one of the two people I know (Jeanne Stawiecki is the other) who has run a marathon on all seven continents and climbed the seven summits (the highest peaks on all seven continents). We ran the Inca Trail together in 2004 and met again in Luxor, Egypt, just that past February.

"I work and live in Jeddah, Saudi Arabia, and I usually take a few days off work for a longish weekend to run the Luxor marathon," Scott said. "It's not a big marathon, and scrolling down the entrants' names, I noticed Don's name there. We had a good reunion; I was with my wife, Suzette, who also runs. Don didn't stay long, as he told me about his world record attempt and he was zooming off either that evening or the next day, early. I was surprised to see Don for the second time that year in Beirut."

It was a cool and comfortable morning as the Lebanese National Anthem played, followed by the starting gun. The first 5K was a spectator-friendly run around a park, back past the starting line. There was water every 2K or so, with separate Gatorade stations as well, and we were fed bananas and dates several times. A young Lebanese guy ran alongside for about 6 miles before we parted company, and I was pretty much on my own for the next few hours.

By the 16K mark, the field had stretched out to where there were no runners visible ahead of or behind me. Fortunately, the length of the course was marked with a traditional blue line of paint, so I would not get lost. At around the 18K point, we started a long out-and-back section. The lead vehicle came through just as I arrived there with the race leaders close behind, about 11K ahead of me. We continued on to Golden Beach, made a 3.5K loop around a very large parking lot, and started back toward the city.

On the way back, however, water suddenly got scarce, and the cool morning temperatures had given way to about 95 degrees worth of heat by 10:30 a.m. Bottles of water and Gatorade that had been at every aid station weren't even available at some. However, many runners had discarded mostly-full bottles along the way. Necessity took precedent over concern about germs, and I picked up the partial bottles to stay hydrated. It proved a prudent move, since the next time a fresh bottle of Gatorade became available was around the 32K mark.

Just past 35K, we headed up an incline called "Horror Hill" on the course map. As is usually the case, the hype was worse than the reality. In fact, the gradual uphill stretch was a nice relief for legs that had been running on a flat course for so long. The party was starting, continuing through a shopping-district street lined with crowds, food, and music. I picked up a kid doing his first marathon at around 35K, and he stuck with me for about three kilometers as we made the turn that followed the Mediterranean Sea toward the finish line.

At about 41K, I drained the last of a bottle of water and worked to catch a big Polish guy just ahead of me. We ran side by side for a distance, and somewhere between 41 and 42K I looked up at him.

"You're killing me, man!"

He smiled and said, "I speak Polish, German, French, and Russian, but no English."

I laughed, since he had just said everything in English. As we made the turn for the finish line he took off like a shot, and in spite of outweighing me by fifty pounds, I could not catch him.

I finished at 4:57, satisfied with myself for running so well on such a hot day. I shook hands with my Polish friend and congratulated him. Marathon number one was in the books. Again. Six more to go. Again.

That night would allow only a couple hours of sleep before leaving the hotel at 12:30 a.m. for the three-hour flight back to Frankfort, then the nine hours to Atlanta. My total flight time so far was twenty-four hours, not including connecting time through airports. I would be back in the USA for a couple days.

North America: Atlanta, Georgia—November 22, 2007

Until 2009, the Atlanta Track Club held a marathon on Thanksgiving Day. Midweek marathons can make or break a record attempt like this, giving the opportunity to check off another continent without using up a weekend. I arrived in Atlanta late Monday and had a couple of days to rest and explore.

At the race expo in Atlanta, I spotted a wheelchair across the room with a familiar occupant. It was William Tan, from Singapore, that remarkable man I had met earlier in February. I immediately knew what he was up to: Another attempt at the world record. Fortunately for me, wheelchair records are in a different category, so we had no rivalry. It was a great reunion, as we shared plans for how we would accomplish our respective missions. In a couple weeks, we'd reunite in New Zealand. We made arrangements to meet there.

The lovely Francine arrived on Wednesday to join me for the North American leg of my adventure, and on a cool and rainy Thanksgiving morning, we assembled at the starting line. At 7:30 a.m., we were off on a very hilly course to complete marathon number two. It was a small event, around 600 runners, with many more in the half-marathon, which started 13 miles away. By the time we finished, they would all be home eating turkey. The holiday-induced five-hour time limit created enough urgency to keep our legs in motion.

The hills were relentless, and the whole course had very few flat spots. Several hills were given names to make them feel more "friendly." It didn't help. The 2-mile stretch between miles 18 and 20 was a long, gradual downhill, but near the bottom, we looked ahead and saw the hill that would make us pay for the 2 miles of easy running.

A few months earlier back in Grand Rapids while running up a hill in a 5K with 6-year-old Carly, I was coaching her on using attitude on hills. "This ain't no hill. What, this is all you got for hills!?" On the next hill, Francine asked if Carly wanted to walk a little, but Carly looked at her and said, "This ain't no hill, Mom," and blasted up it so fast we couldn't catch her. At the top, we laughed when she turned back to look Francine in the eye and said, "Nice job, Mom."

So as we started up the biggest hill of the day, I turned to Francine, smiled, and said, "This ain't no hill, Mom." We smiled and renamed it "Carly Hill," and on the way up, we ran one our best miles of the day, passing many runners who by that time were just trying to drag themselves to the top. The attitude boost kept us passing people throughout the rest of the course. The finish line was in the 1996 Summer Olympics stadium and was my second Olympic stadium finish of the year. At 4:42, it was about fifteen minutes faster than in Beirut.

We never did find any turkey that day, but we enjoyed a nice post-race dinner and recovery before parting ways on Friday. She headed home to Grand Rapids, and I boarded another trans-Atlantic flight back to Frankfurt, en route to marathon number three.

Europe: Florence, Italy—November 25, 2007

Taxis are regulated in Florence, so negotiating wasn't necessary, but due to a bad exchange rate, it cost about $50 for the drive to my hotel. No matter; it wasn't about bickering with cabbies. It was about running the Firenza Marathon that Sunday, November 25.

Florence may be one of the most beautiful places in the world. Somehow, while wandering around the streets trying to find how to get to the race expo, I happened on a group of runners getting on a bus, so I got on with them. It proved a good move, and following the group off the bus, I ended up right where I wanted to be. Sometimes, things just flow the way they're supposed to.

The next morning, I followed the stream of runners and found the shuttles to the race site just a few blocks down the river from my hotel. The whole day was like being in a painting. The city is a blend of beautiful architecture, artwork, and pastel shades, and the soft blue sky was a perfect complement. At 9:20 a.m. the race started. The 4:45 pace team, their red helium balloons bobbing above them, crossed the starting mat just ahead of me.

During the marathon, I ran back and forth with a bunch of the same people, including a couple named Graziano and Nicoleta (their names were on the back of their shirts) until about the 20K mark. After 15K, I encountered food stations with bananas, two-bite chocolate pies, and—for the first time in my experience—little ham sandwiches. Well, I don't know if it was the ham sandwich or the chocolate pies, but around the 19K mark, the bullshit levels in my blood spiked (I'm prone to that), and my pace picked up. Just past 21K, an inflated arch marked the half-way point at 2:19:12. The 4:45 team was ahead of schedule by a couple minutes, and not quite as far in the distance as before.

Something in my brain figured a negative split was within reason, i.e., finishing the second half faster than the first. The extra gear I needed kicked in, and at 31K, the red balloons of the 4:45 pace team dropped behind, never to be seen again. After a long loop around a beautiful park along the River Amo, the course turned toward the finish near the 34K. My legs were still feeling great, carrying me past runner after runner as we worked our way toward the finish line.

Approaching the 39K, each kilometer passed by faster than the previous one. Kilometer 41 was the fastest split of the day until I hit the 42K. With only 195 meters to go, my legs wouldn't quit. It was my third marathon in a week, and the fastest with a time of 4:36:13. The second half was very satisfying—nearly two minutes faster than the first. Endorphins were running high, and leaving the race site, I reunited with Graziano and Nicoleta. We found a warm drink and relived the day's experience together.

The next day was a relaxing recovery day spent walking around the city, taking pictures, and enjoying a beer and pizza at La Borsa Ristorante. Florence streets are lined with statues and sculptures, many of which were already old when America was discovered. The narrow stone streets and alleys form a maze that made it easy to get hopelessly lost, only to dump me back out into a familiar square or walkway. Little cafés and shops lined the streets with many opportunities to enjoy fine Italian hospitality.

My original plan for marathon number four the next weekend in Port Elizabeth, South Africa, went something like this: Fly to Cape Town to spend a few days with my North Pole travel companion, Hans VanEerden. While in Cape Town, I planned to knock another item off my list by going cage-diving with great white sharks off the coast before driving across to Port Elizabeth for the marathon.

Unfortunately, my flight out was canceled due to a very dense Italian fog (really tempted to use that old bigamist joke here), so I trekked back to the hotel, checked back in and spent an extra day in Florence. The next day's flight was rescheduled to leave from Bologna instead of Florence, so a train trip through the Italian countryside was a pleasant addition to the itinerary. From Bologna, it was back through Frankfurt and on to Cape Town, where I would spend a night with Hans before going over to Port Elizabeth for the Aspen Pharmacare Port Elizabeth Marathon, to be held that Saturday. The sharks would have to wait for a future trip.

Africa: Port Elizabeth, South Africa—December 1, 2007

When I arrived in Cape Town, Hans' assistant Kim was at the airport to take me to Hans' villa where his wife, S'jane, met me for a tour that included a couple wineries. She dropped me off at Kirstenbosch Botanical Gardens to see the Bob Dylan Hard Rain exhibit and wander the grounds while she picked up her boys from school. We headed back to their house to meet up with Hans.

Hans and I had only met once before, on a trip to the North Pole in 2003. The fun part of "adventure destination marathons" is that before you finish a trip, you are friends for life with your travel companions. Hans and I had shared the first North Pole Marathon trip together. We had eaten whale meat, drunk beer from the northernmost brewery in the world, peeled frozen layers of skin off our noses, and were part of the first sixteen people to run a marathon at the North Pole. The shared experience forms a permanent bond between us. Several of my best friends are from marathon adventures.

Hans and S'jane had an art function that evening, so they dropped me off at Table Mountain, where I could take the cable car to the top and look down on the Cape of Good Hope, the dividing point between the Atlantic and the Indian Ocean. I watched the sun set over the Atlantic Ocean for my first time. We met for dinner in a nearby market district and caught up on stories. The next morning, Kim took me back to the airport for the trip to Port Elizabeth.

By the time I arrived in Port Elizabeth, I had exceeded fifty hours of flight time, but at least I was in position for marathon number four. A new friend I met in Beirut, Norrie Williamson, had contacted Jan and Irene VanEeden to tell them I would be there, and I promptly got an invitation to stay at their house, which was only a half-kilometer from the race site. South Africans, it seems, are some of the most hospitable people in the world.

After arriving at Jan and Irene's house, Irene directed me to the nearby Kragga Kamma Game Park. Before even entering the park, an enormous ostrich came up to check me out as I was driving up to the admission booth. Around the first bend stood four giraffes, seemingly looking at something off in the distance. Around the next bend were white rhinos, followed by a herd of wildebeests. The whole park was one group of animals after another. Gazelles, zebras, warthogs, you name it.

In the middle of the park was a cheetah enclosure. Double gates guarded the entrance and exit, with a sign that read "Do not open if there are cheetahs between the gates." Duh. During my drive around the short loop, not one cheetah greeted me. *This is not fair. I'm going around again.* The second time, around the backside of the loop, two cheetahs walked out in front of the car and flopped down on the road in the shade. They decided I could wait a while. Finally, I revved the engine a little bit and they got up. Rapidly rolling the window up at that point seemed the prudent move.

The Port Elizabeth City Marathon began at 5 a.m. on December 1 with overcast skies. In South Africa, they take their cutoff times seriously, so my primary goal was to finish under the five-hour cutoff. Finishing faster than in Florence and lowering my overall time for the fourth straight marathon was in the back of my mind as well.

The event had only about 340 runners. License numbers, mandatory for all runners in South Africa, were sewn front and back onto singlets. South Africa has a club system, with runners joining clubs, getting an annual license, and usually dressing in club colors. Foreigners buy a temporary license, which was mandatory with my entry fee. A small tag was given to us to pin to our shirts to turn in to the timers at the end of the race.

Even with a previous marathon only six days earlier, I felt strong. Approaching the halfway point, it occurred to me that with the way I was feeling, another negative split was possible. It was getting warmer, but I felt good and was running steady. At 21K, my split was 2:17:20. That would put the half-way mark at about 2:18, more than a minute ahead of my Florence time.

OK, Marathon Don, let's see what you've got.

I kept my pace and didn't spend much time with refreshments. Every three kilometers came another aid station, serving water in little plastic sachets and small glasses of Coke. I carried packets of energy gel with me and used one about every hour. With about 9K to go, at 3:35:28, I had no time to goof around. At 38K, fatigue was setting in, but turning the next corner thinking how it would feel to say "Two negative splits in the same week" drove me forward. Breezing through the final aid station just before 39K and grabbing a sachet of water, I set my sights on a runner a few yards ahead.

Relax your legs and run, Don. Don't slow down.

I encouraged other runners on my way past them, trying to find someone to pace with to the end. There were no takers. On the final turn toward the finish line, I hit the gas with 200 meters to go, crossing the finish with a time of 4:34:47. First half: 2:18:00. Second half: 2:16:47. Yes! It was my second negative split of the week, and I was the first American finisher in the race. (The *only* American finisher, but it's not my fault you didn't show up.)

Jan and Irene had the official timing company of the event, so getting documentation of my time was easy. We cleaned up and relaxed for a while, and then they took me with them to a family dinner party that night. The time to relax was pleasant, great family time with my new South African hosts. There would be a lot of travel in the next few days, so time at home was wonderful, even though it was someone else's house.

On December 2, I left for the Port Elizabeth airport, but not before buying a set of carved rhino bookends at an open-air bazaar. Hans picked me up at the airport in Capetown, and we feasted on crayfish that he and his boys had caught while diving earlier that morning. After spending a final night with Hans in Cape Town, he deposited me once again to the Cape Town airport for a journey to New Zealand.

Oceania: Wanganui, New Zealand—December 8, 2007

At 10 p.m. Tuesday night, I found myself spending an unexpected night in Auckland before heading south toward my next destination, as my luggage had decided to take a later flight. By noon the next day, however, I was off to Wanganui for marathon number five.

New Zealand is a rugged and beautiful country. Ancient volcanoes worn down by millennia make up the lush green hills and valleys. Herds of cattle and flocks of sheep dot the countryside. The trip was on two-lane roads with small towns along the way, driving on the left side with the steering wheel on the right and a standard transmission. Natives could tell an American was driving because when I wanted to turn, the windshield wipers came on.

Fatigue had set in by the time I reached the small town of

Taumarunui, where I snoozed from 7 to 8:30 p.m. before heading out for a bite to eat. Getting over jet lag had become hopeless, but fortunately the time was mine to just eat, sleep, read, or anything else whenever the body felt like it.

In Wanganui, I located the race organizers and somehow figured out where William Tan was staying. We met for dinner on Friday night before the marathon, comparing notes on our journeys and preparing for the race the next morning. Contacting the local paper, I managed to get an interview and my mug shot in the daily edition the day before the marathon.

On December 8, the early start for the marathon for walkers and slower runners was at 6:30 a.m. With a 1 p.m. flight being the only way out of Wanganui, I took that option instead of the general start at 7:30 to avoid cutting it too close. Four loops of about 10.5K each took us through parks, looping around, over, and under three different bridges, and back through the starting line. The terrain was a combination of grass, gravel, and paved paths.

The week after South Africa should have had me feeling more rested, but the fatigue of nearly three weeks of traveling was setting in. The strength, felt during the previous couple marathons, wasn't as noticeable. Knowing that finishing in time to make my plane was critical, however, I pushed through the fatigue and stayed strong.

The lack of kilometer markers made it difficult to maintain a regular pace, and there was no sports drink on the course for the first two loops. With only water for nourishment and nothing in my pockets to eat on the course, I felt a little depleted. Then, about 3K into the third loop, I found a little baggie of chocolate pieces some unfortunate runner had dropped. At least now I had a little more energy to burn. The lift from the chocolate spurred me on my way. The next aid station had finally acquired some sports drink, so my much-needed stores were getting regularly replenished.

With about 10K to go, time goals were out the window. Finishing was the only priority. Finishing in 5:03 left enough time to grab a shower at the boathouse near the finish line before heading to the airport.

The Wanganui airport is a tiny building, and the agent at the desk looked at me and addressed me by name as I approached. With only about a dozen people on the outbound flight, it was an easy call. After checking everyone in, he walked us out the back door to board the plane. It wouldn't have been much of a surprise if he had gotten in the cockpit to fly us to Auckland, but he left us at that point.

William in his wheelchair had finished before me and was already waiting at the airport. The flight north to Auckland and the subsequent international flight to Santiago, Chile, left as scheduled, and we soon arrived on yet another continent, South America.

Back in February, Richard Takata had denied me the world record partly because he figured out you can run a marathon west of the International Date Line on a Saturday and run one east of it on Sunday, taking advantage of going back to the previous day on the way across. Seems like a guy as smart as me would have figured that out.

So, William and I briefly travelled back in time to Friday before watching our second sunrise that Saturday out the window of an airplane. At the Santiago Airport, my ever-faithful friend Paul Ruesch met me with the Antarctic gear he had informed me about back in Beirut. After a quick switch to a bigger rental car, William joined us for the drive to Viña del Mar, Chile, for the December 9 Costa del Pacifico Marathon.

South America: Viña del Mar, Chile—December 9, 2007

The starting line required a 30-mile shuttle ride from the hotel that housed the marathon headquarters, which made for an early start to the day. Fortunately, none of us had body clocks that even cared what time it was any more. We watched the wheelchair athletes start, with William quickly cruising into the distance and out of site.

A girl we talked to on the shuttle started with Paul and me, and the three of us stayed together for the whole race. The early miles were hilly but not especially steep or difficult. In spite of running in New Zealand only the previous day, the recovery had gone well, my body feeling rested and strong right from the start. While my legs were a little sore, it wasn't bad.

The weather was perfect, overcast with comfortable running temperatures. We made our way through beautiful farm country, then through a large industrial area where mountains of coal were used to generate power. A runner familiar with the local industry explained how the ash from the expended coal was taken across the road to another plant to be used in cement. Sand from the area was turned into glass at another plant we soon passed.

As Viña del Mar approached in the distance, we enjoyed breathtaking views of the ocean to our right, heading south along the coast. Everything was on schedule, and marathon number six was moving rapidly toward completion. At the 42K mark, I called the lovely Francine and put her on speaker to share the final 195 meters with her. She was excited to take the call and asked how it went.

"I didn't finish," I said, teasing her a little bit.

As she started to ask what happened, she heard the follow-up: "At least not yet."

Paul and I talked to her as we approached the finish line, sharing the moment with my sweetie over 5,000 miles away.

After cleaning up, we picked up William at his hotel, and Paul drove us back to Santiago to the airport. Paul went off to explore Santiago before heading home to Chicago, leaving two aspiring world record holders to await the flight south to Punta Arenas. There we would join a group of extreme athletes for the last leg of a very long journey, the Antarctic Ice Marathon.

In the wee hours of the morning on December 10, 2007, as we arrived at the tiny Punta Arenas airport, flashbacks to another adventure-of-a-lifetime filled my head. It was a little like returning home.

Nearly six years earlier in January 2002, a group of strangers had gathered at that very airport. For the first time in history, six runners would attempt to run a marathon at the Geographic South Pole. I was one of those six.

The interior of the White Continent is perhaps the only place on earth less visited than its coastal areas. It may also be the most inhospitable place on earth. On that January day in 2002, we were little prepared for what would happen in the following days.

Chapter 7

The South Pole Marathon, 2002 or What to Expect When Traveling to the Most Inhospitable Place on Earth

///

Snow two miles deep. Wind chill 50 below zero. It would be the adventure of a lifetime. We'd sleep in tents at the South Pole. The adventure we were about to share would be more than we bargained for. It was the first time in the history of the earth that such a feat would be attempted, and the second I heard about it, I knew I had to be there.

A couple decades earlier while watching TV, I saw a man walk around the world at the South Pole. It took him a few seconds. A conversation with a friend from the 1997 Antarctica Marathon one evening in 2001 renewed that memory and prompted a call to a man destined to become one of my best friends.

In early 2001, I got word that Brent Weigner (that's pronounced "weener," as in "hot dog") was trying to put together a marathon on the interior of the Antarctic continent. He had contacted Adventure

Network International and convinced them that running a marathon at the South Pole was a good idea. Brent and I didn't meet in person until we arrived at the airport in Punta Arenas, Chile, on January 2, 2002.

A couple other "recurring characters" in my running career would join us on the trip as well: Richard Donovan, who would later become race director of the Antarctic Ice Marathon as well as the North Pole Marathon, and Dean Karnazes, who was not yet a phenomenon but was working on his first book. He hadn't yet become the international cover model described by some as "the fittest human being on the planet."

I like to refer to Richard and Brent as my bi-polar friends, by virtue of the fact that the three of us have been to both poles together.

On a summer (in the Southern Hemisphere) day in 2002, we would embark on an adventure that would be nothing like we expected. Originally, the trip was advertised as an eleven-day adventure, with the caveat that we could expect some delays. Perhaps that was a bit understated.

December 31, 2001: After months of continuous preparation, it was finally time to depart. What a journey it had been to get to this point. Acquiring the necessary gear for this trip took six months. I searched the Internet and watched sales to find the right combination of equipment to keep me safe and warm in the most inhospitable environment on earth. I picked up my last pieces of gear the day before.

I spent most of the weekend organizing gear, and after repacking a couple times into one of those huge army duffel bags, I finally got it all in. The only problem was it weighed nearly 60 pounds. As I wrestled my load onto the scale at the airport, the nice lady checking my luggage looked up and said, "I think that's oversized." She took out her tape measure to confirm her suspicion. Only $80 extra to ship it to Miami. In Florida, I spent my last night in the United States with my mom and dad, taking a trip to Wal-Mart to pick up another piece of luggage. I was repacking as we rang in the New Year.

January 1, 2002: I could handle all my bags at once as I checked in for the overnight flight to Santiago, Chile, then on to Punta Arenas.

January 2: In spite of never meeting Brent Weigner in person before, we recognized each other immediately at the Punta Arenas airport and were already good friends. One of our guides, Bean Bowers, met us at the airport. Six "clients" plus Bean, the driver, and everybody's gear but Brent's was piled into a little van, and we headed into town. (Brent's luggage took a later flight.) Our trip was scheduled to take us to Patriot Hills on January 4, where we would spend two nights, fly south to a spot 26.2 miles from the South Pole, wait two more nights, run a marathon on January 8, and then work our way back to Punta Arenas on January 11.

Bean's briefing in the van told us otherwise.

"There's a group that's been waiting for a weather window since December 21, and they're due to fly south on the next flight," he said.

That's right. They were twelve days behind. We would have to take the second flight. Brent and I were roommates at the Calafate, a little hostel. We went out that afternoon for some cerveza (beer) and lunch, and while at the café, we met Klaus, a climber from Germany who would be on the Dec. 21 flight. He was extremely unhappy with Adventure Network International (ANI), the tour operator that does all of the tourism to the interior of Antarctica and was the organizer of our trip.

Brent said he initially liked my "zeal for life and importance of having a 'bucket list.'" Those happen to be two qualities he also admires about himself, so it only figures those are two reasons why we hit it off so well.

Not that Brent is one to beat around the bush, of course.

"Don is arrogant. So what? Many successful people I know have some of that quality," he said. "It kind of goes with being a mover and a shaker. I used to tell my students there are three kinds of people in the world: those who watch things happen, those who make things happen, and those who wonder what happened. Don makes things happen."

Really, Brent? Me? Arrogant?

January 3: We got up a little late this morning, around 6:30 a.m. or so. There was nothing special to do, so we worked to condition ourselves to take life at a slow pace. We hooked up with a climber named Stu to go for a run in the Magellan National Reserve, a ten-minute cab ride from town. The ranger pointed out a 2-mile route marked by red-topped posts that led to the summit of a small mountain by way of a pasture full of horses (and their byproducts) and a trail through some woods.

We started the run under sunny skies in the crisp, cool, early summer air. As we approached the exposure on the summit, we met the same strong winds that permanently deformed the trees near the ridgeline. As the trees bent away from the wind, we leaned into it, powering our way to a summit that rewarded us with a great view of the city of Punta Arenas and the Straits of Magellan. We continued on the trail through a copse of trees covered with Spanish moss and on to a logging road before turning around.

On the way back, the sunny sky turned rapidly to clouds, and before we knew it, we were running in a rain shower. After only a couple minutes, we were running in snow. The weather changes very quickly in Tierra del Fuego (the Land of Fire). The snow lasted only a few minutes, though, as we continued back to the ranger station to meet our taxi driver for the trip back to town.

At 7 p.m., we had a briefing for the marathon runners and crew. It looked pretty good for the group that had been waiting since December 21. The earliest we could leave was January 5. Everything depended on the weather. Before we could fly, the conditions at Patriot Hills had to provide a good visual contrast between snow, clouds, and sky to land planes on the blue-ice runway, and winds could be no more than about 20 knots.

At this meeting, all the runners met for the first time. The marathon runners included:

- Brent Weigner, age 52, from Cheyenne, Wyoming.

- Ute Gruner, 55, from Bonn, Germany. Ute is one of the strongest women I have ever met. The previous year, she skied across Greenland, and the year before that, she skied the last degree to the North Pole.

- Raphael (Rafi) Rottgen, 29, a German investment banker living in London, about to transfer to New York.

- Dean Karnazes, 38, from San Francisco. He worked for a biotech company, but his real passion is endurance athletics. He is a member of The North Face adventure team, and the company sponsored him for this event.

- Richard Donovan, 35, an economist from Galway, Ireland. His only previous endurance event was the Marathon des Sables. He is also a member of a running family, a brother of former NCAA champion runner Paul Donovan.

- Don Kern, 45, from Martin, Michigan. That's me.

The staff included:

- Bean "I'm just a snowmelter" Bowers, a mountain guide from Wyoming. Bean proved a great mentor and friend on this trip.

- Doug Stoup, expedition leader for ANI. He had just finished a trip where five clients skied the last degree to the South Pole.

- Kris Erickson, photographer and mountain guide from Montana.

- Duncan Gray, a Scottish expedition doctor from Glasgow.

- Devon McDiarmid, a guide from Whitehorse, Yukon, whom we later met at Patriot Hills.

We received backpacks from The North Face, hand warmers, Clif Bars, GU, Wigwam socks, and some Aloe Up products. After the briefing, somebody (perhaps me) suggested that since we were just sitting around getting acquainted, perhaps the conversation could move down the street a short distance to be continued over some cerveza. A very, very short discussion ensued.

January 4: We had a big briefing in the morning with everyone waiting for our flight to Patriot Hills. The marathon was only one of four different adventures represented here. One group was going to hunt meteorites in Pecora, a few hundred miles from the Pole. There were two separate groups climbing Mount Vinson, and several who were going just to see the South Pole.

We found out the marathon would end about a half-mile from the Pole, so there was not much chance I would get to run around the Pole naked following the race (darn it). Oh, and between the first flight and ours, a fuel flight was necessary, so at that point, we were on the third flight to Patriot Hills.

Brent, Rafael, Richard, Dean, and I took a taxi back to Magellan National Reserve to run the trail again. This time, we went farther, then followed the posted trail to the other entrance of the park. If I turned my head the wrong way, the wind at the top of the ridge nearly blew my glasses off.

As we approached the end of the run, we came onto a quarter-mile stretch of thick moss. Running behind Rafi, I watched as his feet sunk deep in as they hit the moss and then like a spring flew back into the air, the moss bearing no trace from the force of his steps.

January 5: Since we had at least two days before proceeding south, Dean, Brent, and I rented a car and drove north about four or five hours to Torres del Paine (Blue Towers) National Park. We chased guanacos, ran some trails, and enjoyed a tremendous buffet at the hotel there. Dean and Brent headed up the mountain the next morning, with Dean running all the way to the base of the towers. I stayed closer to the hotel and hiked the trails with my camera.

We arrived back at the Calafate late that evening to find that our stuff had been packed up and we were booked at another hostel about a mile away. After much confusion, we arrived at our new accommodations and worked to sort out our gear. Brent had to go back to the Calafate the next day to retrieve parts to his computer that had been left in the dresser. All part of the adventure.

January 7: Two days earlier, the group that had been scheduled for December 21 finally went out. The fuel flight went one day later, and it looked as if we might head out on today's flight to Patriot Hills. We spent the morning packing bags, getting briefings, and talking to press people. At about 5 p.m., we were picked up and transported to the airport for a flight on a Russian Ilyushin airplane to Patriot Hills.

January 8: Around midnight, our plane touched down on the blue ice runway near the camp at Patriot Hills. Because they couldn't just hit the brakes on the ice, we rolled for what seemed like miles, slowly coming to a stop. The door opened to some of the freshest air in the world. We hauled our gear nearly half a mile to the Patriot Hills camp, set up tents, and had a short welcome session in the dining hall. The temperature was around 0 degrees Fahrenheit, but with twenty-four hours of daylight, the tents stayed comfortable all night. Jamie, the Patriot Hills camp manager, gave us the first morning briefing at our temporary home, and we again learned that the advertised itinerary was quite different from the actual one.

A DC-3 would take us to the starting line of the marathon. First, however, it had to take the "Pole baggers" to the South Pole and back. Then it would deliver a load of equipment to Pecora for the meteorite group. Then the meteorite group would follow on the next flight. After that, the marathon could go on, since the DC-3 would stay with us as we completed our mission. In other words, we now were on the fourth mission to fly out. Our two nights in Patriot Hills would be a minimum of four, and that was if the weather cooperated. And since today's weather was not cooperating, the plane sat on the ground. This was originally scheduled to be the day of the marathon.

The only permanent building at Patriot was an underground (undersnow?) plywood hanger where ANI's Cessna was stored in the winter. After breakfast, several of us went down there for a workout and did pull-ups on a couple frog-shaped climbing holds put up by Alex Lowe, the well-known mountain climber.

At 7 p.m., we were live on a Fox Sports radio show, which interviewed several runners. We also did the first of our daily dispatches for Doug's Web site, IceAxe.tv, which we did most every day during the trip.

January 9: Today, the weather improved. The first flight to the Pole went out early, and it looked as if the Vinson climbers would go out in twenty-four hours in ANI's Twin Otter.

In the morning, we went for a snowmobile ride out to an ice lake about five kilometers away. The ice was clear, and as we looked down into it, we saw an irregular honeycomb of ice crystals, starting at the surface and extending down out of sight. A few feet away, bubbles rose from the bottom, getting bigger as they approached the surface, frozen in the blue ice. Rocks, some as big as three or four inches across, had blown off the adjoining mountain and surrounded the lake. We ran back to camp, where Dr. Duncan hooked us up to an EKG and checked our pulses and oxygen levels.

We ate well, even getting beer and wine with dinner. We also stayed nice and warm too. Daylight 24/7 kept the inside of the tent reasonably "warm." I slept in only the inner bag of my double sleeping bag, wearing a light shirt and shorts. A sleeping mask made it dark enough to sleep.

At the briefing, it looked good to head south tomorrow or the next day. We've learned, however, that patience is not only a virtue here, but a necessity. We were at the mercy of this vast, beautiful continent. We were also at the mercy of the ANI time schedule.

January 10: The group of Pole baggers came back at about 1 a.m., mission accomplished. Jonathan Silverman of Ft. Lauderdale, Florida, had become the youngest person to ever reach both poles, at 11 years, 6 months. He felt pretty good about it too.

The night was very warm in the tent, so we opened several vent zippers. An hour later, though, the weather turned cold, and we zipped up our sleeping bags for a change. It doesn't take long to get cold when the sun goes behind the clouds.

Several years ago, a DC-6 crashed in whiteout conditions about 6 miles from there. We took a trip out there, where only the tail fin still protruded out of the snow. Brent, Richard, Raphael, and Dean ran all the way back. Ute and I came about halfway back with the snowmobiles and then ran the rest of the way in. Ute's English was passable, but she didn't have a real good grasp of American colloquialisms. After Dean passed us with a "Hi, guys!", Ute waited until he was out of earshot, then asked me, "What does that mean, 'Hi, guys!'?" She and I became good friends on this trip.

When I returned to the tent to change out of my running clothes, I looked down and noticed Brent's bottle, labeled "PISS" in big black letters, totally empty. A couple feet away at the far wall of the tent was his water bottle, full of something that looked like apple juice. Good thing he didn't get thirsty early that morning.

The Vinson climbers got out on the Twin Otter, and the plane full of gear for the meteorite people left as well. It looked as if the meteorite folks would go the next day, and we would follow shortly after. Patience.

I got a little exercise here and there by shoveling snow while waiting for the bathroom, which always needs shoveling out. Everything needed to be shoveled out on a regular basis. Our tent was about half covered with snow, and we had to clear out the entrance every time we went in or out. Ute's tent next to ours seemed to be trying to bury itself. She had a straight-out entrance, and somebody had to dig her out every morning.

Dean, in spite of his tremendous athletic ability and experience, had little experience running in cold weather. On the way in from the DC-6 crash, he had stripped down to just one pair of tights for a while. When he stopped to relieve himself, he found that a certain part of his anatomy had no feeling at all. Everything was better in a few hours, but it gave him quite a fright. It also gave the rest of us interesting material for writing limericks in the dining hall that evening.

That afternoon, the winds increased, so we spent our time at the dining hall writing in journals, reading, and talking. At 3:18 p.m., we got a briefing from Doug. It looked like it would be at least two days before we could head south.

January 11: Winds were at 20-plus knots with gusts to 30. We waited for the meteorite folks to fly out so we could go. Weather was not good at the Pole, so it was uncertain whether anyone would fly. The weather report indicated a system was forming off Queen Maud Land, and it was anybody's guess which way it would go. Activities after breakfast included digging out the tents and packing all the marathon gear for the bivouac-tents, food, and survival gear.

Dean, Richard, and Rafi had used some snow blocks left by the Vinson climbers to build snow walls around their tents the previous afternoon. By morning, the high winds had blown the snow in around the walls and nearly buried their tents. We spent a while dismantling the walls and digging everyone out.

During a 9:30 a.m. briefing, it looked like we would try to get the marathoners out as far as Thiel Mountains, where ANI has a refueling station. There was a storm, and we would try to beat it. At the very least, we could start the acclimatization process there, and the DC-3 could pick us up and take us to the start after it delivered the meteorite group to Pecora.

During lunch at 3:30 p.m. we got the word that weather at the Pole was bad, but we could spend one or two acclimatization days at Thiel. We spent the last two hours breaking camp. The Twin Otter had gone south to check on the weather, and if it was okay, we planned to head out in the DC-3 in about an hour.

At 4:30 p.m., we went out to the DC-3 and started to board when we heard from the Otter that the weather wasn't good. We waited another half-hour, but at 5:30 p.m., the mission was scrubbed. Bad weather. We had to spend the night here again and then try again the next day. Winds had picked up and blew very hard. Our staff arranged for us to stay in the library and the one Weatherhaven tent instead of erecting all the little tents again.

January 12: Thiel was socked in, and it looked like it would be for a couple days. We may be here for a bit.

It got cold last night when the clouds rolled in. Dean had a hard time keeping his feet warm while sleeping.

Richard pulled his leg a little while dismantling the snow walls. Dr. Duncan took good care of him, and the interaction between a Scottish doctor and an Irish patient gave us quite a few laughs. Duncan played the diabolical doctor who takes pleasure in the pain of his "Irish potato" patient. The good-natured banter lightened the mood, a pleasant diversion from the constant waiting.

We took a snowmobile trip to Windy Pass in the morning. Standing in the pass, we looked down on the ocean-blue water, with a white-sand shoreline reaching up into the mountains. But the water is blue ice and the sand is snow. We ran back to camp from there, past the Chilean government station. It was abandoned for the season, and we could look in the windows and see the various rooms. The station was built like a series of bubbles joined to form long tunnels, with only the top third rising above the snow's surface.

Any problems we had were minor. We were fed well and stayed warm except when we chose to do otherwise by going out in the snow and playing. There were many things to do if you looked around a bit. Rafi and Duncan, with the slightly injured Richard supervising, built a little igloo near the edge of camp. We worked to keep our spirits up, but impatience grew, and we wondered how much longer it would be before we could get on with our adventure.

January 13: We had now slept six nights here, and we became way too accustomed to it. Rafi reported that the environment affected his dreams. He had visions that he was at his parents' house and they surprised him by coming home unexpectedly from a trip to Antarctica because the weather was perfect and all the flights were early. That's right, Rafi, you were dreaming.

My gear worked well. My wife, Nancy, had made some neoprene gaiters that fit down over my shoes. They kept my feet toasty while running. The neoprene mitts we made for running were very light and warm.

At 11:20 a.m., our weather report briefing was delayed for nearly two hours. Here was the deal: the weather at the Pole was good, and Thiel was clearing. They would watch closely, but the plan was to send the meteorite folks out at about 12:30 p.m. on the DC-3. Assuming that went well, the plan was to send the runners next and then Doug and Duncan out on the Twin Otter a couple hours later. Kris, Bean, and Devon would join us when the DC-3 became available. If it all worked, we would run the marathon early that Wednesday, return back here by that night, and fly back on the first flight back to Punta Arenas. Everything, of course, depended on the weather.

Meanwhile, Richard's knee felt much better, and Dean's feet warmed up well. Brent and Dean went out for some short runs. Richard, Rafi, Ute, and I hung out around camp, waiting to see how much the news would deteriorate.

At 7:30 p.m., it did. At 2:30 p.m., the meteorite folks had been put on hold until at least 7 p.m. Now they were back in camp with the mission scrubbed. A new Weatherhaven tent was set up, and Dean, Ute, and I had a great space to sleep, with real beds with two mattresses on each one and lots of space to spread out. Ute saw the two mattresses stacked on her bed and exclaimed, "Die Prinzessin auf der Erbse." (The Princess and the pea.)

Ute's husband had hired a trainer, since this would be her first marathon. For several months, she had gone without alcohol and sweets and had planned to do so until after the marathon. Before too long, though, we managed to corrupt her just a little bit. Chocolate was readily available here, and she really enjoyed it. She also found that a bit of red wine with dinner made it easier to fall asleep when the winds threatened to blow our tent away.

More information about what actually can and can't happen kept trickling in. It turned out the maximum weight the Twin Otter can hold is far less than we were told when we made plans earlier in the day. The only way we can do the marathon is with the DC-3. Misinformation was quite prevalent, and many times, it felt much more intentional than it should have been.

January 14: High winds and overcast skies meant no one would fly out that day. I played a couple games of Scrabble in the morning, intentionally staying out of any of the discussions rampant among my fellow "clients." Debate and discussion about options, contingencies, and who had to go home and when continued throughout the morning. Tempers were on the edge of exploding, but everyone managed to keep things under control. Crew members tried to figure out plane payloads, pilot schedules, and what scenarios might play out. Mostly, we felt helpless, with no control over what would happen next and no way to just stuff it and go home.

Back at the "Patriot Hills Hilton," Dean and Kris did some upper-body workouts, so I joined in for a while. At around 2:45 p.m. on the way to the igloo to see if anyone was hanging out there, I saw Doug shoveling out the Cessna hanger. Stopping to help him for a few minutes turned into a great hour-long workout. Another hour passed in an endless stream of white hours.

By evening, the sky had cleared, and the wind died to nearly nothing. Many of us headed outside to take pictures or generally goof around. It was a calm, quiet night for sleeping.

Evening, night, morning, day. They're all terms we use to describe *when.* But not in Antarctica. They merely refer to the time on our watches, which were set to Chilean time. The reality was that all the time ran together in a constant stream of daylight hours, the sun making lazy circles around the sky, never going below the horizon in any direction. Constant daylight.

January 15: Eight nights in Patriot Hills, and we'd probably just enjoyed the best one so far. Ute and I decided we would run the marathon together. She wondered, "What if I can't finish?" but she would probably do great. She's very strong, and we'd just approach it one marker at a time until we found the finish line.

The weather looked good at the 9:30 a.m. briefing, both at our camp and at the Pole. The meteorite crew was headed out the door to break camp. The pilots probably wouldn't be back here until around 1 a.m., so the earliest we could go out would be early the next afternoon. At least we were next in line. Rafi, however, had a tough decision to make. He was set to start a new job in New York in early February, and all the uncertainty made things difficult. We even discussed running a marathon here so Rafi could do one before he had to leave, if it came to that.

At 9:30 p.m., we took snowmobiles over to Windy Pass and hiked the ridge along the mountains past the camp. The backside of the mountains was made up of layer upon layer of sedimentary rock, pushed up into short mountains that form the Patriot Hills. Climbing up one of the faces, we traversed the thousands of layers of rock deposited year by year many millennia earlier. Walking up and down the mountain, we were traversing the earth's history. Our hike lasted three hours, and we walked back across the blue-ice runway to camp.

The DC-3 headed south at 12:16 a.m. We were next on deck.

January 16: Our ninth morning in Patriot Hills. Morning briefings grew tedious, with an expectation of disappointment replacing the hopefulness we previously had. The weather at Thiel was bad, and the Pole was tentative. Both locations were needed, the refueling at Thiel being critical to getting us to the Pole. It would again be at least evening when the next satellite picture came out at 6 p.m. "What if" scenarios of how to get to Thiel, to the starting line, or to who knows where, buzzed through the dining tent. Just to get this marathon under way. Emotions ran higher every day. Maintaining my "It's all part of the adventure" attitude was getting difficult.

January 17: Decision time. It was good weather for flying, and we were headed for the Pole. Max, the pilot, gave us a briefing and let us know we could be camping near the South Pole for up to two weeks if the weather turned against us. It was great to have such a confidence booster.

As we once again gathered our belongings to prepare for the trip south, Rafi made the tough decision not to risk the extra time away from work; "I'm 25 years old and have a job that allows me to take a trip like this. I'm not going to risk it." There was no talking him out of it, and our number dropped to five. Ute was next to reconsider, and she came back to our Weatherhaven tent crying, not knowing whether she could take the time either. Bean came and talked to her, and she started to come around. After Bean left, the two of us talked, and I assured her all of us were scared, but we were with a great crew of guides and I believed we'd be safe. There were a few more tears, but she decided she had to go with us.

Wheels up at 12:45 p.m. We were finally on our way south. After two hours, we stopped at the fuel dump in Thiel. The Thiel Mountains are a small range, and the landing strip is a flat area within view of the mountains, marked with black garbage bags filled with snow. Other than the black bags, the only other signs of mankind were 55-gallon drums of fuel and a Canadian flag. After an hour, we were airborne again, and at 5:33 p.m., we landed at the South Pole. Doug headed in to Amundsen-Scott Station to find out where we would be assigned space to set up our tents when we returned after the marathon. The rest of us ventured out to take pictures and bask in the realization that we were at the southernmost point in the world.

It was a warm day at the South Pole, -13 degrees Fahrenheit with a -58 wind chill. The extreme cold was more than most of us had ever experienced. The view was crisp, white snow—flat, desolate, bare in all directions as far as the eye could see, broken only by the station buildings. We had little idea how dangerous this could really be.

We left Bean and Devon with snowmobiles so they could mark the course on the way out to us, then reboarded the DC-3 to fly to the starting line.

Max found a tentative landing site and did a couple test touch downs to make sure the wheels wouldn't sink into the snow. Finally, he put the plane on the surface, and we began setting up the camp.

Our "southern camp" would be a communal twelve-foot dome tent that would serve for melting snow for drinking water and cooking. We would sleep in two-person North Face tents. Our latrine was a short wall of snow blocks, a bucket with a toilet seat, and a stake in the ground where we would urinate to keep all the pollution in one spot. The solid wastes would be carried out with us later. Thankfully, frozen.

"Once we were flown onto the Polar Ice Cap, around 10,000 feet above sea level, it was seriously cold," Brent said. "-35 to -40 degrees Fahrenheit plus wind chill put the temperature around -50. After that, we referred to base camp at Patriot Hills as the banana belt."

Max had landed us a couple miles from where the race would start, so we were camping about 28 miles out and would have to be shuttled to the start by snowmobile. By the time we set up camp, melted snow, and made supper, it was after midnight. The elevation was around 9,300 feet. Five runners, five guides, and a three-man flight crew would sleep the next three nights here to acclimatize before running the marathon.

We had no idea where Bean and Devon were until about 3 p.m., when the call came in over the radio. They had snowmobile problems and ended up camping at the 14-mile mark.

January 18: Like at the Pole, the vista was the same. White plains and blue sky in every direction. Here, however, there were no buildings, no activity, and nothing but flat, white desolation. Duncan created a little "café" by digging out snow blocks and piling them up on the windward side of a pit, with a table in the middle and a bench all around. My winter gear was warm as I sat sheltered on the bench, and soon I was enjoying a nice snooze.

January 19: Devon and Bean finally came in overnight, having set out all the course markers that would count down our journey to the pole 1 mile at a time. Because Doug was filming the event for his website, IceAxe.tv, we held an "official" start at 3 p.m., a made-for-TV event with banners, pictures, and video, followed by some individual action shots and interviews. The actual start would be the next morning.

Following our little media session, Bean gave us a short talk. "It's best to treat this as an expedition instead of a race. Always leave 10-percent in the tank in case of trouble, because it's one of the most dangerous places on earth."

Bean Bowers was one of the most reassuring people on the trip and was instrumental in keeping us safe. His common sense and experience were strong. He was a mountain guide and a good friend to have in a bad situation. He left us that day with a strong sense of self preservation, forcing us to realize that surviving the adventure was by far the most important aspect.

Dean had a great assortment of gear, including some he helped design for The North Face. He meticulously tried on one combination of clothing, running a mile or so, then another and another, working hard to get his various systems "dialed in." Whether that invoked envy or relief is hard to know; having only a small amount of gear to manage seemed a lot easier to me.

The course was designed to take us on a straight line, approximately along 80 degrees west longitude. The miles counted down from 26 to the finish line, about a half-mile from the South Pole. Originally, the Cessna was to be down there with us, leapfrogging with the DC-3 to set up aid stations at 20, 15, 10, and 5 miles from the finish. But instead, we only had the DC-3, and a runway was set up at the 14-mile mark so we would have an aid station there. To make it safer by keeping us close together, Ute and I would start at 6:00, Brent and Richard at 7:00, and Dean at 8:00, with the hope that by the time we were 12 miles into the run, we'd all be close together. That's where the DC-3 would set up an aid station, 14 miles from the finish line.

January 20: Race day. It was partly sunny and looked promising, and Ute and I were taken the 2 miles to the starting line by snowmobile. Doug would stay with us for the first 6 miles and establish an aid station at the 20-mile mark. We had to wear packs with some extra clothes and a down jacket, and carry some food and a water bottle, a total of 10 or 12 pounds. It was about -25 with a little wind. We sank into the snow up to six inches with every step. According to ANI, the nearly 10,000-foot altitude at this latitude feels more like 12,000.

We started at the 26-mile marker, and by the time we covered the 1.2 miles to the 25-mile mark, more than thirty-five minutes had passed. The miles were taking us about a half-hour. It would be a long day. Then it got worse. The partly sunny skies faded to gray, and the air around us filled with an icy fog. Doug went ahead to a mile marker to wait for us to come by, and we would drink and eat a little.

As we progressed past the 24-mile mark, it became obvious we weren't doing a smart thing. After waiting for nearly three weeks to get the race started, it was clear that if the weather persisted, we couldn't continue. Disappointment started to set in as I realized what was coming.

Passing the 24-mile mark, we had a hard time seeing the marker wands in front of us. We almost reached the 23-mile mark where Doug waited with water and food. Visibility was failing, and the whole world had turned to milk. Everything from ground to sky was completely white. We fought to see where to go next, wishing the wands were closer together. Ahead of us, as Doug turned around on the snowmobile to tell us the race was canceled, the horizon disappeared in a ghost-like world through his slightly fogged goggles. He was a pilot lost in a fog, not knowing which way was up. Soon he lost his equilibrium and fell off the snowmobile.

While enjoying a good laugh at his expense, the danger of the moment didn't escape me. We were 5 miles from the plane, 23 miles from the Pole, there was no visibility, and temperature and wind chill figures were well into the double digits below zero. The race we had waited for so long was over. Doug picked us up, and we headed back.

Within a mile, the snowmobile—bogged down by three people and a sled full of gear—stalled out. We needed to lighten the load. Doug figured I could drive Ute and myself back to camp, then send someone out to get him and the sled.

"Are you comfortable with that?" he asked.

"Not really."

That turned out to be my best decision of the day. He tinkered with the snowmobile for a few minutes, and it ran better. We found Brent and Richard near the 25-mile marker and told them to head back, then went on. We met Kris on the other snowmobile out around the 26-mile marker and sent him to get Brent and Richard as we headed back to camp. We set out across the frozen landscape to cover the distance to our tents, but after riding for about ten minutes, we found Kris back at the 26-mile mark. We had been driving in a circle and were back at the starting line. We were over 9,000 miles from home, lost and freezing. Equipment wasn't working right, guides were confused, and if we needed help, the possibility of it reaching us on time was slim.

If a guy were prone to getting nervous, this would have been the time. Fortunately, none of us were, except maybe Ute. What an adventure!

Brent and Richard had arrived back at the starting line by that time so, with everyone back together, we all loaded onto the two snowmobiles and sleds. Kris had either a better sense of direction or a better GPS unit, and we followed him back toward the plane, stopped by only one more episode of the snowmobile stalling out.

The white of Antarctica faded to a gray funk as we considered the events of the past few weeks and the dismal outlook. Finishing a marathon in these conditions could be more dangerous than I had bargained for. Carrying a pack at this altitude and in these temperatures, it could take me fifteen hours.

Maybe we could try again the next day, but the weather didn't look promising. Brent talked to his wife Sue and apparently felt pretty low, too, not knowing whether he could finish such an event. Sue and my wife Nancy talked and emailed, and when we did the iceaxe.tv dispatch, Nancy had left me a message: "Use your head. Don't do anything stupid."

January 21: The wind outside announced we wouldn't run, so my sleeping bag got some extra use. Ute woke up and said, "Call the plane. I want to go home now."

Several things had become clear to most of us. First, this is a much more dangerous event than we first thought. Second, even with the quality of our guides, the ANI staff could not adequately support all five of us to guarantee our safety. Third, the weather can change from good to bad so quickly that the slightest bad decision or mechanical problem could mean severe problems or even death. We spent the whole morning, as well as much of the previous day, running scenarios, plotting, and figuring how we could make this event happen. We had to make it happen, one way or another.

Here is what we came up with: Brent and Richard would wear the only two pairs of snowshoes we had, and Dean would wear just running shoes. The three of them would run without packs, supported by both snowmobiles, and would stay close together until the last few miles of the race, pretty much expedition style. Kris and Doug would be with them on snowmobiles. Sleds were packed full of food, hot Thermos bottles, tents, and other supplies in case the weather closed in and camping became necessary. If any of the three couldn't continue at any point, the race would be called off. Ute and I would fly to the Pole and do a half-marathon on an out-and-back course where we could be easily monitored.

My heart's desire was to do the marathon, but there was no way I could keep up with the "expedition." So I swallowed my disappointment and did what had to be done to make it work for everyone. If only three of us could complete a South Pole Marathon, we could still consider the adventure a success.

"Don and Ute deserve much of the credit for the success of the event," Brent said. "They agreed to drop down in distance and run a half-marathon, and that freed up the two snowmobiles to take care of the remaining three runners."

At 4:30 p.m., after more than an hour's delay due to snowmobile problems, they finally left for the start line. Max warmed the plane— about a three-hour process—as those of us remaining packed and broke down camp. We flew to the Pole and put up camp, and Ute and I made our way to the finish line to begin a multiple out-and-back loop half-marathon.

As we ran back and forth on a mile out-and-back course for about the fifth time, Richard came into view, coming in on snowshoes with nothing on his head. I gave him a hug and cheered him on. On my next lap, I met Brent and Dean, running only a few yards apart.

The final results:

- Richard 8:52:03
- Dean 9:18:55
- Brent 9:20:05

Brent and Richard went back out on the course for a couple more miles to complete a 45K event:

- Brent 9:59:53
- Richard 10:10:09

Ute and I did the event in running shoes, and not having the packs made the miles a lot faster than the previous day. Our half-marathon times were:

- Ute 5:48:56
- Don 5:53:00

I changed clothes in the airplane and, in the process, put my thumb on a piece of bare metal super cooled by the frigid air to -25 degrees or colder. Instantly, the flesh turned white, and to this day the feeling in the tip of my left thumb has never quite come back. It's freakin' cold at the South Pole.

After changing, we all went into Amundsen-Scott Station for an introductory talk by National Science Foundation staff members. The station was still housed in the geodesic dome structure containing a small "city," which serves as home to a little more than 200 people in the summer and around 60 in the winter. One room in the dome was a little store, where we bought gifts for the people back home. Doug and Kris even picked up a couple bottles of Glenlivet scotch.

We got back to our camp only a couple hundred yards away around 5 a.m. on January 22. Rather than go to sleep, we waited for the 7 a.m. briefing. I assisted Bean, Kris, Doug, and Duncan in disposing of the Scotch as we waited the two hours for the morning weather report. As usual, it was not favorable, so we spent the day under cloudy skies, resting, eating, taking pictures, and recovering from our run.

January 23: Lyrics from The Eagles' song "Hotel California" ran through my head as we woke for our last time at the South Pole: "You can check out any time you like, but you can never leave." This had been a great adventure, but I'd had about as much adventure as I can stand for one trip.

The morning weather looked questionable but showed promise. By midmorning, the weather became sunny with very little wind. If you've read *Ultramarathon Man* by Dean Karnazes, you've read the infamous Naked at the South Pole story. It just seemed like the thing to do, so Dean and I took the opportunity to take some more pictures by the Pole, this time standing naked behind it. The silver ball atop the striped pole was strategically placed to make the pictures family friendly.

While the pictures froze that moment in time, we were quick to get things done and get back into warm clothes before anything else froze, because, as previously mentioned, it was freakin' cold! Before dressing, I took the opportunity to run "around the world" naked, which Dean credits me with being the first in the world to ever do. Another thing checked off the Life List?

By noon, the weather at Thiel cleared, and we packed up and headed back to "summer camp" at Patriot Hills. We arrived around 6 p.m. to a celebration in our honor, a short awards program, and even champagne in addition to our usual beer and wine with dinner. We took the opportunity to celebrate until about 4:30 a.m., drinking in the dining hall and then cramming ten people into the igloo to finish up whatever was left of the booze and even smoke a couple cigarettes.

January 24: Needless to say, most of us missed breakfast. The day's big goal was a nap, a couple meals, and maybe another nap. It's been nearly three weeks since we've seen darkness. The Twin Otter picked up climbers on Vinson, and the DC-3 headed out to get the meteorite people. There was an outside chance we could be home this weekend.

January 25: We had slept in Antarctica 18 nights. The Ilyushin flight was coming in to get us around 7 p.m. Ten people were waiting to go to the Pole, so they would have to wait for the next flight to get out of Antarctica. A couple blew it off and just went home.

January 26: The Ilyushin touched down in Punta Arenas at about 1 a.m., and we deplaned into the first darkness any of us had seen in nearly three weeks. At the Calafate, the first shower since leaving Punta Arenas was so nice I never wanted to get out. Lying in a real bed with warm blankets and a nice, fluffy pillow with the scent of soap fresh on my body, I inhaled deeply. "Damn, I smell good." Sleep was sweet, knowing the next day we would leave for home.

In retrospect, the decision to do only a half-marathon was good. Dean and Richard normally run marathons in the 2:30 range, and they took around nine hours for this one. I normally run around 4:30 marathons, and I would have been on the course for a dangerously long time had I decided to do the full 26.2 miles. It appeared no one suffered any serious problems, but Richard had some superficial frostbite on several toes and was a bit hypothermic. Even after spending the amount of time I did running a half-marathon, I felt pretty fresh, with no ill effects at all. Our race was nothing like we expected. But the expedition was an amazing adventure.

WOOD-TV 8, a Grand Rapids news station and NBC affiliate, surprised me at the airport along with Nancy and a small group of friends. The last question in the short interview was "Would you do it again?"

Big smile. "Of course I would."

Three years later in early 2005, Outdoor Life Network filmed one of their countdown series on the 25 Most Dangerous Places on Earth. All the way down at number five was the South Pole. The story they told was about the South Pole Marathon, and in the filming, they interviewed Brent, me, and a third guy who was there to basically tell how stupid we were to even attempt such a thing.

Maybe he was right. Maybe he wasn't. But in my life, it still ranks as one of the best adventures ever. Of course, not running a full marathon ending at the South Pole leaves me feeling like I have unfinished business at the southern end of the world.

Chapter 8

The Antarctic Ice Marathon

The 2002 South Pole Marathon experience rolled around my brain on that December day in 2007. William Tan and I took the half-hour bus ride to the Diego de Almagro Hotel in downtown Punta Arenas in the wee hours of the morning on December 10. The experience at the South Pole prepared me for whatever might happen next.

Race Director Richard Donovan had some family situations that year, so he hired Brent Weigner to stand in for the 2007 Antarctic Ice Marathon. So, for the second time that year, one of my best running/traveling companions would share the adventure. We rang Brent's room as we checked in around 4 a.m., and he came down to say hello.

Three hours later, we would leave for the White Continent.

Or not. Brent shared the news from the Ice. A rare storm in the Ellsworth Mountains had the Patriot Hills ice runway blown in.

Climbers had been stranded for days at their climbing base camp at Mount Vinson. Three hours was looking more like three days.

Since the window for good weather was unpredictable as ever, we spent the day shopping and then went out with a few guys for beers and dinner. We ran into a couple of Americans driving motorcycles from Santiago to Ushuaia and then north to Bolivia. An evening of beers and war stories in a faraway land. What a great time to be a guy!

The weather didn't improve the next day. At a meeting that afternoon, organizers from Adventure Network International (ANI) told us it would be at least two full days before we could even think about traveling to Antarctica. The best-case scenario would be running the marathon on December 14, still within the timeframe to set the world record. That was good for a little cautious optimism. But listening "between the lines" to the tones and the qualifiers made me feel like the situation may not be as good as they would like us to believe.

It was Tuesday, December 11, the day before the world record was supposed to fall. Instead, eight of us hired a minibus and driver for a trip to Torres del Paine National Park. It was a long trek but worth the six-hour drive. The area was filled with gorgeous scenery, highlighted by mountains in the distance that became more snow-capped as we approached. Many trees along the way were stripped bare by relentless winds in the area and grew sideways under the constant pressure.

We arrived at the Las Torres Hotel by late afternoon, rented a few rooms, and then gorged on an amazing buffet of fresh salads, smoked salmon, leg of lamb, roast pork, chicken, and beef. The next morning, it was raining sideways, but we hiked the trails anyway before heading back toward Punta Arenas.

When we arrived back at the Diego de Almagro late on Wednesday, December 12, the ANI crew was there. We were still on hold. On Thursday at 1 p.m., we got word we wouldn't be flying south that day. Or Friday. Or Saturday. I had until 4:17 p.m. on Monday the 17th to finish the marathon in Antarctica, or the only world record I would own would be for running all seven continents twice in one year—and that wasn't the one I wanted. I was starting to feel disappointed. There was still hope of flying out on December 16, and almost everyone on the trip was game for running within an hour of when we got off the plane. Everyone wanted to be home before Christmas, me included.

During the afternoon, Brent and I took an excursion to an island to see a Magellanic penguin rookery. Just what I needed. More penguins. I had seen enough penguins to last a lifetime.

Days got lazy. On Friday, December 14, I slept in for a little bit, then watched some TV before breakfast. Bad feelings crept in, along with a few minutes of depression. After a year and a half of planning and running, and after two attempts at the record, I felt a bit discouraged. Something I had worked so hard for was rapidly moving out of reach.

At noon, I went for a run up the hills heading out of town on gravel roads for about 5 miles before turning around. The past month's events replayed in my mind. The great friends I made in Beirut. Winding through the streets in taxis that narrowly—but always—avoided colliding with each other. Dinner at the Palm in Atlanta with my favorite woman in the whole world, and finishing a marathon with her by my side. Being "stuck inside a postcard" in Florence. Hanging out with new friends in South Africa and seeing rhinos, zebras, and giraffes. Driving through the New Zealand countryside. Running a marathon with my best friend Paul in Vina del Mar. Even coming down here, stuck in Punta Arenas with some really great people.

Most people experience nothing like this in their lifetimes. In fact, most people don't even do things like this in their imagination. And this was the second time in 2007 that I would run on all seven continents. As my feet hit the gravel outside Punta Arenas, I underwent a good attitude adjustment. How could a guy feel bad, given all the great things that happened in 2007?

The morning of December 15, Brent and I took a taxi up to Magallanes National Reserve to run some trails. We were last there together in 2002 and found it a great place to run, so we were excited to return. We picked the right day too, sunny and not too windy. We followed a row of orange stakes marking a mountain bike trail through the woods. The trees are mostly deciduous but with small leaves. Big leaves wouldn't stand a chance; the constant heavy winds would strip them bare in a few minutes. Trees are gnarled and twisted, and many are covered with beard-like moss that hangs from the branches.

We followed the trail through the woods as it turned uphill, slowing us to a walk for about half a mile. As we climbed the mountain, we looked down over the town of Punta Arenas and the straights of Magellan. We took a break after our run, and I made a pre-arranged call to my regular running buddies gathered in a coffee shop back in Grand Rapids after their Saturday morning run. I updated them on my situation, and most of them sympathized with my plight.

We returned to the hotel in time for a 5 p.m. briefing. Things looked better at Patriot Hills, and we hoped we'd fly there on December 19. But that sealed my fate. My world record quest would officially fall short. Another briefing was scheduled for 3 p.m., December 18. *Does this hotel rent rooms by the month?*

Before breakfast on December 16, we ran into Vic, a runner staying at our hotel. He told us about a 10K race that was being held later that morning in Punta Arenas, so we grabbed a quick bite to eat and found a taxi. The day was rainy, and we soon found out that while there were a lot of different races, they were divided by age groups, not by choice. People over 51 were supposed to run a 6.5K race. The 10K was, I think, for men only under 50. Vic, Brent and I told them we were running the 10K anyway.

About a block into the run, volunteers diverted "senior division" runners around a corner as the 10K continued straight. Seeing Brent's white beard, they (rightly) assumed he was a senior and insisted he make the turn. So he did. Vic and I continued. (Vic is 67, by the way.) I ran dead last for the first 4K, so I had a motorcycle escort. During that time, four young guys running near me realized they were in over their heads and dropped out. Vic was still in sight and ran steady, knowing I'd catch up sooner or later. Some youngsters lost steam, and I reeled a few of them in.

As we got to the center of town, I finally caught up to Vic, and we ran together the rest of the way. We picked up an adventure racer who had just finished a four-person 1,000K relay in Patagonia, and we ran with him for most of the rest of the race. We hit the finish line at just over fifty-five minutes and were greeted as heroes. They appreciated that we ran the race with them, and somehow they also got wind of the fact that Brent and I were headed to Antarctica. We stayed for the awards but really weren't sure why, other than thinking maybe Brent would win an award in his race. He didn't.

At the end of the ceremony, we were surprised when the three of us, along with one other guy who had recently moved to Punta Arenas for work, were called to the podium. They recognized us for coming, and made a big deal about Brent and me going to Antarctica. They gave us each a small medal and a present: a small running backpack. The local crowd gave us an ovation and we felt welcomed, with many locals coming up to wish us well.

At the 3 p.m. briefing the next day, we were told the runway was being cleared and we might fly in the next morning. At 6:30 p.m., Brent told us to pay our bills and expect a 4:30 a.m. wakeup call for the flight south. Things looked good, but I had been here before. I knew how this could go.

At 4:50 a.m., I got a call from William Tan. "Did you get the phone call?"

"No."

"Me neither," he said. "I guess I'll go back to sleep."

But at 5 a.m., Brent finally called. "Be in the lobby in fifty minutes. Bring your passport." We were going to Antarctica.

Around 7:30 a.m., we boarded the Russian Ilyushin 76 airplane.

This was not your normal commercial flight. The whole plane was open, with no panels on the ceiling and overhead cranes on rails running down each side. Cargo was stacked down the center, strapped down by nets and tarps. A big snow cat was loaded in the back, about the width of a semi-truck. Rows of seats ran along each side of the plane, and we strapped ourselves in for the four and a half-hour flight to the Patriot Hills. The constant roar of the engine lulled most of us to sleep as we flew over the Drake Passage and over the ice of Antarctica.

At 12:40 p.m., an announcement was made: "Get your gear on. We're about to land."

It was nearly a half-mile walk from the blue-ice runway to camp. Steve Jones, the camp manager, gave us a briefing in the dining tent. We had arrived in a world few people will ever see, about 800 meters (2,600 feet) above sea level, and 500 meters of that is snow and ice.

The dining area was a long, Quonset hut tent with a kitchen in the back. It was our home, where we would eat, read, and interact for the next few days. Accommodations were in clam-shell tents, with plenty of room and two beds in each. Compared to 2002, it was The Ritz. Brent and I shared a tent again; by that time, we were used to each other and knew we could sleep in the same room.

There was plenty of sunshine after we arrived, so Brent went out to the runway and marked off a course. Richard Donovan had created a wheelchair category to allow challenged athletes to take part. The rest of us couldn't run for a day or better, so we took turns walking/running parts of the marathon with William, as he became the first person in a wheelchair to complete a marathon in Antarctica. His was a whole different kind of adversity, because while the surface was hard, it was far from smooth, and traction was non-existent.

Instead of finishing in a faster time than most of us without wheels, William spent the time from just after 5 p.m. until sometime around 3 a.m. completing the 26.2 miles. His persistence inspired us all as he became the first man to complete marathons on all seven continents in

First marathon finish, Chicago Marathon, October 1995

First seven continents Finish in Adelaide, Australia, August 1998

Finishing the 50 states, November 2003, with Francine Robinson

The geographic South Pole,
Antarctica, 2002

2003 North Pole Marathon

Running in Luxor, Egypt, February 2007, during first world record attempt (Richard Takata is on the far right)

Finishing second marathon in Luxor

At the summit of Mt.
Kosciouszko, Australia's
highest point

Enjoying the sites in Seoul

Finishing the Seoul, South Korea
Marathon with Paul Ruesch and
Brent Weigner

Florence, Italy, third marathon of second world record attempt

Finish line in Port Elizabeth, South Africa, December 2007

Running in Magallanes National Reserve outside Punta Arenas, Chile, December 2007

Antarctic Ice Marathon, 2007

Knocking William out of his
wheelchair (Not on purpose!)

With Dr. William Tan
(The fastest person on
seven continents!)

Speight's West Coaster Marathon at Bethel's Beach, New Zealand
(The toughest marathon ever!)

Accomplishing the
"impossible" at the Space
Coast Marathon with
Francine Robinson

Finishing the seven continents at the Antarctic Ice Marathon, December 1, 2011

Guinness Certificate for finishing in 25 days, 18 hours, and 10 minutes

a wheelchair. Twice he had tried to do Antarctica on King George Island, but the course and time restrictions stopped him. But now he was a world record holder, not only for the men's wheelchair division, but also for the whole human race, doing all seven continents in less than 27 days.

From William's website: "On 19th December 2007, Dr. Tan became the fastest person in the world to complete 7 marathons across 7 continents in 26 days, 17 hours, 43 minutes, and 52 seconds to raise funds for international charities on 7 continents. His amazing race took him to Antarctica, Chile, Egypt, Thailand, Japan, Kenya, Italy, England, New Zealand, and USA between November and December 2007."

Patriot Hills felt like home. Brent and I had lived there for most of January 2002. The camp had been updated since then. The "ice toilets" were much nicer, with two lined up in a small Quonset hut-style tent with a wall down the middle. All our waste was sent back to Chile for disposal, so we relieved ourselves in numerical order: No. 1 in the urinal, which exited into a small drum, and No. 2 into another toilet. There was a sit-down toilet for women, who then could dump a pee-bucket into the urinal. The solid waste went into black plastic bags that were bundled up and sent back on planes. At night, we kept pee bottles in our tents to avoid having to bundle up and go out.

"Night" is a relative term when the sun is up twenty-four hours a day. We ran our clocks on Chilean time, just to keep us in sync with the people back at ANI headquarters.

All our water came from melted snow. A big pile stood outside the cook tent, and we shoveled it into tubs and carried it in to melt in a large metal bin near the stove. We always had lots to drink, whether it was hot water, cold water, or juice in big coolers. The kitchen staff was amazing. Every meal had lots of variety and was very well prepared. We also had snacks—chocolate, cookies, dried fruit—available all the time.

The weather wasn't looking too promising—again—and since organizers still had to groom and mark the course, we knew we wouldn't be running. Two feet of fresh snow, more than normally falls in a whole year, had wiped out the trail they had prepared the previous week, so they were forced to start from scratch. After grooming the trail, it needed to freeze over and solidify before we could run on it. They were optimistic, though, that the marathon could start first thing in the morning.

The next day, at 7:12 a.m. on December 20, we started the Antarctic Ice Marathon. To prepare, runners sent snacks and extra gear out to the three aid stations. I decided to carry whatever I needed in the small backpack from the 10K in Punta Arenas. It was windy and about 10 degrees Fahrenheit as we started the race. Before the start, my toes were already cold in spite of the heavy wool socks inside my running shoes. I started at the back of the pack but gradually caught up with some runners as I settled into a nice pace. Constantly flexing my toes to push off the slightly grainy surface soon warmed them to an acceptable level. After far too many days of rest, it felt great to run again.

We followed little flags and the tracks of the big caterpillar that had been driven over the course to mark it. The surface had solidified quite well in the previous eighteen hours and was relatively firm. Still, at every footstep, the surface of the snow gave way under the pressure of toes pushing off, loosening under our feet, shortening the length of every stride. It would be slow going all day.

Looking at the Patriot Hills from the camp, we would proceed to the left for a first loop around the end of the small mountain ridge. We ran out of camp, keeping the mountains on our right, toward the first aid station tent about five or 6 miles out. Even that short distance seemed long. Finally, after an hour and twenty-two minutes, I arrived to find that only about half a cup of melted snow water was available. They told us someone would be along on a snowmobile soon with more to drink.

A mist of snow was falling, and before the first aid station, the icy precipitation had deposited a glaze on my glasses. The beautiful course we had been promised was obscured by a milky white fog, leaving us unsure of where we were at any time.

I pulled out a sleeve of cookies from my pack while leaving the aid station and ate a couple as the mountains shifted between us and the camp. We were between two mountain ridges at the time, isolated from the camp and nearly everything else on earth. Low visibility and poor contrast kept us constantly vigilant to find the next orange flag.

The wind had shifted to our backs, and soon sweat was accumulating in my base layers. Sweating too much in cold conditions can lead to real problems as wet clothing freezes, leaving one encased in ice. I took off my outer wind jacket to allow the sweat to move through my clothing instead of pooling in my sleeves and soaking my gloves as it ran out. Wicking the sweat to the outside, it froze on my sleeves and was easily brushed off.

After nearly an hour, the promised snowmobile arrived with some hot lemonade. I didn't drink a lot, though, because I was told the next aid station was only about 2K away. As it turned out, that estimate was a bit off. After a while, the trail curved around to the right and headed slightly uphill through a pass in the mountains. Nearly an hour after seeing the snowmobile, I finally reached the next tent. I drank a couple glasses of hot liquid but had to be very careful to avoid burning my mouth. Now the course headed back toward camp.

Sweat continued to freeze and keep my shirt stiff. Still, I was comfortable as long as I kept my legs in constant motion through the loose snow. Camp should have been visible by that time, but with the fog and low-contrast conditions, I couldn't see. I ran, alone in a world of white, with only a couple runners in the distance in front of me.

At around 11:15 a.m., I could make out camp. About fifteen minutes later, I arrived at the finish banner after taking nearly four and a half hours to complete the first 27 kilometers. Still feeling fresh and strong, I went into the dining tent, drank four glasses of "juice" (orange-flavored sugar water), scarfed down three cookies, and went back out before my outer layer thawed. I actually passed three people at that point by keeping the stop short. We headed out of camp for the final loop, away from the Patriot Hills toward a DC-6 plane that had crashed a few years back. The contrast worsened, and in this direction, there were no mountains for landmarks. Only white. Lots and lots of white.

I struggled to see the trail and frequently wandered off to the side, only to sink into the snow. Because the loop was long and narrow, we could occasionally see other runners heading back toward the finish, letting out a whoop and raising our arms to encourage one other. We were too far apart for words, but the sentiments were felt. Susan Holliday, who was running the 100K, and I had teamed up for most of the loop, so we worked the course together, searching for flags that would lead us all the way to the finish line. Finally, after an hour and a half, the final aid station tent came into view. After a brief stop, we made the turn for home.

Heading back toward camp, the wind picked up, blowing snow into our faces from the left. The markers were even farther apart and harder to spot, but I knew the finish line was ahead. More and more often, I wandered off the side of the track, sinking into soft snow and then correcting course. Colorful specks appeared in the distance, becoming tents and then people. As the finish line came into focus, exhilaration set in. I raised my arms and crossed the line after seven hours and twenty-eight minutes of running. Basking in the moment, I stood under the banner for a short photo session.

William was there in his wheelchair, and I went over to give him a hug. Unfortunately, I seriously misjudged the stability of the chair, and the next thing I knew, we were both flat on our backs, lying in the snow laughing like lunatics. People tried to help us up, but William waved them off and said, "Take a picture."

I had just finished running marathons on all seven continents for the second time that year. It was a new personal record, finishing in just under 33 days. It wasn't what I set out to do, but still, it was very satisfying to finish the circuit. It was also my third completion of the seven continents. Brent is the only one on the planet who's run all seven continents more times than that.

With the mission done, we waited at Patriot Hills Camp for the proper weather conditions for transport back to Punta Arenas. As soon as it was suitable, the Ilyushin would bring in a load of fuel for the camp and take a load of passengers back. Everyone was anxious to return home for Christmas, speculating on the weather, wondering about the logistics to clear the runway, get the plane here, and get us back out. But Antarctica isn't like anywhere else on earth. There are no scheduled flights. We were at the mercy of the weather and the logistics to get us out of here. We would go home when the continent allowed us to go home.

Finally, after a three-day wait, we were able to return to Punta Arenas. From there, it was an overnight flight to Dallas. The lovely Francine met me at Gerald R. Ford International Airport in Grand Rapids at about 3 p.m. on Christmas Day. My mission was complete. No, I didn't make the world record as planned, but I did accomplish a few things. I took two days off my own personal record, completing the seven continents in a little less than 33 days. I also was the only human on the planet who had run all seven continents twice in one year.

While running around the globe, I knew something even better waited for me at home. No matter how far away I get, people who love me back home are still there.

Life is wonderful. Sometimes I wonder if I'm in a movie or something. If that's the case, my character has some great writers. And while I'm hoping they leave out future scenes where I knock guys out of wheel chairs, I look forward to what they'll come up with next.

Guinness doesn't list everything in their database, but perhaps they could think about something like this:

MARATHON ON EACH CONTINENT TWO TIMES - MEN

"Marathon" Don Kern (USA) completed a marathon on each of the seven continents twice in 307 days between February 16 and December 20, 2007

***

That morning I called my buddies back home, after Brent and I had been running at Magallanes National Reserve, several of them shared my disappointment. But my good friend, Dr. Bob Camp, had quite a different perspective:

"I don't feel sorry for you. Not one bit! You've travelled around the world twice in one year, and now you have an excuse to do it again."

You may have something there, Bob.

Chapter 9

Transitions and Adversity

After running a personal record two-dozen marathons in 2007, the lovely Francine and I headed to Florida to start 2008 at Disney World with The Goofy Challenge—a half-marathon on Saturday followed by the full marathon on Sunday. It was a fun event, with finishers earning a Donald Duck medal for the half-marathon, a Mickey Mouse medal for the marathon, and a Goofy medal for those "goofy" enough to do both races on the same weekend. We made it even a little more challenging by running the family 5K the day before with Carly, and, of course, spending the afternoons on our feet touring The Animal Kingdom and Epcot Center.

Meanwhile, after my last experience in Antarctica, I decided the best chance to achieve my world record would be at the Marathon Tours Antarctica Marathon, held in February or March. Because they sell out a year or two in advance, I registered for the 2009 event, to be held more than 13 months in the future.

On a Saturday morning near the beginning of February 2008, however, something happened that threatened to take me out of the game. It was during one of those Michigan winter runs on crusty, irregular, thawed-and-refrozen roads. A slip, a slide, or some misstep torqued my left knee in the wrong direction. Although it didn't feel unusual at the time, the first few steps of the Sunday morning run were an adventure in pain. Something was wrong. I took a few days off, but things didn't improve. Most of the training during the next few weeks was on the flat indoor track at the YMCA, running short distances.

I had a marathon streak going at that time. The Disney World Marathon was my 59th consecutive month of running at least one marathon. Running a marathon once a month wasn't a critical thing, but I was having fun and wanted to continue the streak. So, in February, to round it out to an even five years, I ventured down to Dublin, Ohio, for the Last Chance for Boston Marathon, a 1-mile loop around an office park repeated 26 times. The Last Chance for Boston, set up at the end of February, was so named because it was the end of the Boston Marathon qualifying period. It was the original déjà vu race. Only one aid station (or 26, depending on how you look at it!) and lots of repetition as we cross the timing mat 26 times. My finish time was slower than normal, and something was still wrong.

In spite of the injury, I worked my way gingerly through a marathon each month to keep the streak alive. Things seemed to improve, and at the Bayshore Marathon in Traverse City, Michigan, at the end of May, it seemed I was on the mend. But the following Tuesday while running hills at lunchtime with friends from the YMCA, the pain suddenly worsened. Over the next couple weeks, I received physical therapy from my good friend, Terence Reuben, and improved. Then one day while he worked on my knee, he tested the joint with just a little pressure. He instantly read my short, quick breath and the grimace on my face.

"I think you might have a torn meniscus," he said. "We should have Ed take a look at this."

Dr. Ed Kornoelje is my good friend, and his office was just down the hall. He and I met for the first time in May 2004 at the race expo for the Fifth Third River Bank Run, a major 25K race held annually in downtown Grand Rapids. Dr. Ed and Terence are the driving forces in the Metro Health Sports Medicine Department, the medical providers for the Fifth Third River Bank Run. At the race expo, Dr. Ed approached me about helping with medical coverage at the inaugural Grand Rapids Marathon, scheduled to take place on Halloween that year, less than six months away. The relationship grew into a sponsorship, and by 2007, Dr. Ed and Terence had talked the people "upstairs" at Metro Health into being the title sponsor of the Metro Health Grand Rapids Marathon. My marathon.

Fortunately, if anyone could understand the meaning and weight behind my personal marathon goals, it was Dr. Ed, himself a runner.

"His knees had been getting sorer and sorer. He started to have some pain in his calf, so he came to see me," Kornoelje said. "I told him his calves may be tightening up, but I thought it was his knees that are really the problem and the calf was bearing the brunt of that. We did some X-rays, and he had a little bit of arthritis, which is not unusual. But then we did an MRI, and he had a meniscus tear. The problem here is that it was just not going to get better. It was just going to get worse and worse."

If there were ever guys who could get a runner back on the road as quickly as possible, Ed and Terence were the ones. Dr. Ed ordered an MRI, which was performed in the middle of the night on July 1, 2008. Even with the impending July 4 holiday weekend, Dr. Ed made a call and obtained the results a few days before they would normally have been available.

On the morning of Monday, July 7, Dr. Ed called me into his office and confirmed Terence's suspicion. He had also made an appointment for that afternoon with Dr. Peter Theut, one of the best orthopedic surgeons in town, who specializes in Sports Medicine. Dr. Theut has worked with athletes of all ages and abilities, whether it's consulting athletic trainers at area high schools and colleges, or working as the orthopedic team doctor for the Grand Rapids Griffins, an American Hockey League team that is the minor-league affiliate for the NHL's Detroit Red Wings. He has also worked with the Grand Rapids Rampage, the City's former Arena Football League team.

I met with Dr. Theut who confirmed Ed's assessment of severe arthritis in both knees, especially below the kneecaps. The area had turned to bone-on-bone to go with the meniscus tear in the left knee. Dr. Theut's first opening for a knee scope was that Thursday. I handled it like I did the first time I heard of the Antarctica Marathon—I knew it needed to be done, so why hesitate?

"Let's do it," I told him. "One question, though. I've done at least one marathon every month for 64 consecutive months. Is there any chance I can run a marathon this month, on the 27th?"

I assured him I was willing to drop out if it didn't work, but I hated to mess up the streak. The good doctor just looked at me, smiled, and shook his head. I took that as a "yes."

As I told him about my passion for running, I'm not sure he realized just how serious I was about staying in the game and keeping the streak alive. Dr. Theut said he tells most people to take it easy for the first several weeks and not to attempt vigorous exercise for at least four to six weeks. (The doctor who did my vasectomy gave me similar instructions. I may not have paid much attention to him, either.)

After the surgery, getting up off the gurney in the recovery room, putting my feet on the ground with the help of a couple attendants and a pair of crutches, it was immediately apparent that things were better. Flexing the knee, everything felt properly aligned for the first time in months. It was truly an easy recovery as well, with only a couple days on crutches and only one pain pill taken as a precaution that first night. By the following Wednesday, running a mile on the track at a YMCA caused only minor discomfort. It was slow and easy, but it was fine.

I reported for a post-op checkup after twelve days and told him I had run 7 miles over the weekend and 4 miles already that day. They may not have been my best runs, but there were no ill effects.

Sixteen days after getting up off the operating table, I was in Carrollton, Michigan, at the starting line of the Carrollton Charity Road Races Marathon. It was slow, and with a low mileage base I ran out of steam and walked most of the last 6 miles. But in 6 hours, twenty-eight minutes, and a few seconds, my streak was alive, my knee wasn't swollen, and another marathon was in the books.

Before 2008 ended, Dr. Theut would perform arthroscopies in both my knees about three months apart. He made a few small incisions and inserted a small camera into the joint. He made a separate incision as an entrance point for the instruments used to clean up the tears and arthritic debris. That first operation in July was unexplored territory for me but Peter Theut's area of expertise.

"Like most folks, I told Don to take it easy for the first several weeks," Theut said. "He told me he was going to push it and start running as soon as possible. Usually if people ignore our advice in that regard, they quickly realize the knee swells up and is painful until healing is allowed to take place. I thought he would probably try to do too much too soon and then realize he had to slow down. That is not really what happened at all."

Amazingly, Dr. Theut said the knee looked great. No swelling, no irritation, no anything. In the two months prior to the second scope, I had even run three marathons. Dr. Theut said he had never seen a faster recovery. Not that he would recommend that kind of "recovery" again.

"At first I thought he was a bit crazy and would realize pushing that hard that soon was just not smart," Theut said. "He certainly proved me wrong. I was amazed at his ability to recover quickly and run marathons on knees that were already pretty severely damaged before the surgeries."

Dr. Ed Kornoelje disagreed. "I knew what his goal was and didn't think it was nuts. It would be one thing if he had some sort of ailment or injury or illness that could cause life-altering problems, but this wasn't that sort of thing. Even in the medical community, there's a lot of talk about wearing out your knees and running, but if you look at the studies, people who run have fewer problems with their knees than those who don't. I was fully expecting when he came to see me that he would want to keep going. We certainly don't recommend that everyone does this, but he had a special thing going, and there wasn't any reason for him not to try to do it."

My marathon times were slower than before, but it was still fun, and the adversity just made the stories better. August, September, and October brought four more marathons. Then, because the left knee was such an easy fix, I decided maybe the right knee, which had been feeling like something inside it wasn't quite right since 1995, could use some attention. It wasn't a specific injury; it really just needed cleaning out. My deductible on my medical insurance had been met for the year, so two days after the 2008 running of the Metro Health Grand Rapids Marathon on October 19, it was time to get the right knee done.

I recover from this stuff like it's nothing, I thought. The first surgery had given me a sense that recovery would be as easy the second time. A false sense, it turned out. Several nights awake with pain, and a few extra days on crutches and a few painkillers were a rude awaking. Fortunately, my next scheduled marathon wasn't until toward the end of November.

As I questioned my ability to recover enough to go for the record book one more time in 2009, changes to the Antarctic Treaty—the agreement that governs tourism to Antarctica—reduced the number of people who could run the marathon there the next February. Many of us were bumped to the 2010 trip, a welcomed move that would allow more time for sore knees to heal.

The year 2008 came to an end, and the dawning of 2009 brought new questions about the future of my marathon career. My traditional New Year Resolution is to have at least as much fun in a year as I had the previous year. It occurred to me that 2008 was the first year in a long time that the resolution had been broken. In fact, during a very slow marathon at the end of December in Springfield, Missouri, I found myself busy making plans to retire. Maybe get to 100 months in a row and then call it good. The streak was at 70 as 2009 started. Long runs were tough, and my knees hurt after every one. Thirty more seemed possible, but they just weren't as fun as they used to be.

Throughout 2009, there were many ups and downs. A fairly good marathon would be followed by a couple that seemed to go on forever. Sore knees and more recovery time followed every bit of progress. There were more rest days and fewer training days. Just to be safe, I told Marathon Tours to postpone my Antarctica trip to 2011. Throughout 2009, I plodded through seventeen marathons and moved my streak to 82 months. Still, my marathon career wasn't as fun as before. Would I ever be able to go after the world record again? *How many paper clips would have to be chained together to get into Guinness?*

The Wall

Marathoners are well acquainted with "The Wall," that place in a marathon where your body wants to give up and your brain is thinking it's a good idea. If I ever hit a wall in my marathon career, the winter of 2010 was the time. It had been well over a year since the second surgery, and the constant nagging pain along with slow running times wore hard on my resolve. Marathons had become less of a joy and more of a chore. The streak kept me going, but my heart wasn't in it like before.

Finally, in March 2010, after running a particularly tough Ocean Drive Marathon in New Jersey, I got aggravated. The five and a half hours running on a cold, rainy, windy day gave me lots of time to think. I made a plan. I'd take the whole week off to rest and heal.

A week later on Sunday, I ran an 8-mile tempo run on a measured course, trying to stay steady the whole time. Monday through Thursday, I ran 3 miles each morning at 5 a.m. on the YMCA track. Each day brought a 15-second decrease in the time for 3 miles. I was training my legs to turn over faster. The next Sunday, the Martian Marathon in Dearborn Heights, Michigan, yielded a 45-minute faster time than only two weeks before. Was it the road to recovery? Times weren't as fast as before, but the quick improvement was a real kick in the attitude.

As the marathon calendars were filling in for 2011, plotting the world record attempt around the Antarctica Marathon began. I still wasn't sure I was ready, but I had to take a look. Trying to find just the right combination of locations and timing wasn't working either— getting all the continents in under 30 days was a lot tougher than I had hoped. Having a ten-day commitment in the middle of it for a boat ride to Antarctica made it even worse. The plan was elusive, and finally giving in to disappointment, I sent another notice to Marathon Tours and moved the attempt to 2012.

During 2010, though, marathons began to be fun again. My knees improved, and I finished in less than five hours more often. In July, I completed my 200th marathon with John Bozung, the guy who put the seven continents idea in my head back in 1997, as he finished his 300th marathon in Salt Lake City, Utah. Later in the summer, traveling to Omaha, Nebraska, I finished running marathons in each of the 50 states for the second time. Marathons, while not as fast as they were before, felt good again. I had broken through the wall. Marathon Don was back.

Another year, 2011, started well, and as the year progressed, the 2012 marathon calendar developed. The Antarctica Marathon was being held on March 9, which eliminated a couple great opportunities in early February, when marathons in northern Africa were scheduled for a Friday and a Monday, making a weekend double with Europe possible. The Oceania and South America schedules weren't working well either, with the only possibility for the Date Line crossing being so far from an airport it wasn't feasible. As the realization set in that 29 days or less wouldn't work, I talked to my old friend Brent Weigner on the phone.

"(Richard) Donovan moved his date up to November 30 this year," he said. Again, the question popped into my mind.

I wonder what the schedule looks like around the Antarctic Ice Marathon?

Gentlemen, start your search engines.

Chapter 10

My Life as an Instigator

A long, long time ago, a couple young boys were playing with a ladder in a sand pile, and they found out it would reach high enough to lead all the way to the garage roof. After taking in the view from the top, the older boy climbed down first, leaving his kid brother stuck up on the roof after taking away the ladder.

"Jump!" the older brother yelled, which was met with a quick refusal. "Come on, it's not that high. The sand is easy to land in."

Truthfully, at about 12 feet or so, the garage was four times as tall as the kid on top. And sand isn't a very soft surface. But who does all that math at six or seven years old?

After a few more minutes, the younger sibling gave in, hitting his chin on his knee as he landed in the sand, bleeding a little bit and crying, but no broken bones or anything. My little brother, Tom, didn't have anything wrong with him that wouldn't heal up in a couple days. Unfortunately, he was hurt enough to tell Mom.

Well, Mom was livid, and I got my butt whooped pretty good that day. Lesson learned. Instigate, but don't hurt anybody. Got it. Now what could I come up with next?

A few decades later, the instigator was still active, and the seeds were planted that would one day grow into a major sporting event in the West Michigan area.

The Shawn and Don 5K

It all started innocently enough. I was drinking a beer with my Grand Rapids Running Club buddy Shawn Sweet at Founders Alehouse one Friday night in November 2000. Shawn was having an IPA, and I drank Amber Ale. There on the table, we saw it—a card advertising the "Second Annual Stout Release Party." It sounded like good, innocent fun: a pint of stout, a T-shirt, and a small buffet. Ordinarily, I could resist such temptations, but after a tough three-day workweek and a couple Ambers, I yielded to the pressure and slipped the card into my pocket.

Later that night, a brainstorm hit. I emailed Shawn: "A T-shirt, a beer, and some food. The only difference between that and a 5K is a run. How about making it the Shawn & Don 5K?"

His quick reply: "Where do you come up with this stuff?"

Shawn and I had been running together for a while, and we were becoming pretty good friends with both of us enjoying the combination of exercise and a decent microbrew. It was only natural to meet back at the scene of the crime to conspire as to how we would pull it off. We used a measuring wheel (a piece of equipment I just knew I would need some day when I bought it) to plot our course, and we found that by going under the bridges on the river walk in downtown Grand Rapids, it was possible to run a 5K without ever crossing a street. An easy and elegant course. Or at least we could advertise it as easy.

"Don and I would have a pint of beer, go for a run on the Grand River from the Sixth Street Bridge down to Fulton Street and back, have a beer at Founders, sit around, and say it was fun," Shawn said. "We figured why not invite some friends and whoever wants to come down and run down by the river and then have a beer?"

Clandestine emails were sent to unsuspecting runners. How many could we draw into our little web of intrigue?

We scheduled the event for Friday night, December 9. The beautifully paved bike path along the river was, by then, buried in more than a foot of snow. As the runners sat freezing in their cars, I marked the trail through the snow with orange chalk. Only the smartest among us knew to just go into Founders and have a beer while the more adventurous lined up at the starting line.

After an easy start on paved streets, the fun began. Down by the local fish ladder, the going got rough. A false sense of security vanished as runners plunged through knee-deep snow along the path by the river. Gates were closed along the trail, which forced intrepid racers to go over, under, or around. Three sets of stairs, buried in snow, made the running treacherous.

At 22:48, our winner, drinking buddy, and sometimes sidekick Kevin Holmes came in to the cheers of, well, nobody, since the smart ones had decided not to wait out in the snow. Soon, Dan the bandit (an unregistered runner) came in, then our first-place woman, Libby Jennings. The rest of the crowd soon showed up, and Lee Nee, perhaps only a little taller than the snow drifts, crossed the line and dropped into the snow bank, exhausted but happy.

Shawn's wife, Joyce, and her friend, Jane, started late, so Shawn and I waited for them to (finally) cross the finish line. Jane lost her racing virginity at this race and figured any 5K in the future would have to be easier than this one. She and Joyce finished in around forty-eight minutes.

Everyone who started the race finished. No blood, no broken bones, no hypothermia. Ten runners participated, with at least ten more joining us for the fun afterwards. We found Founders Stout very smooth and easy to drink, by the way. After a couple pints, we left very happy.

The first Shawn and Don event was in the books.

"We were always looking for fun things to promote the (Grand Rapids Running) Club and also help out local charities," Sweet said. "We would get together and say, 'Why don't we do a fun run?' For instance, we did a sock run for the veteran's hospital in Grand Rapids, and the entry fee for the race was a six-pack of socks. We tried to do novel things that just stood out, and when you do things like this, word spreads around the community pretty fast."

The Frogger 5.5K

December progressed, and another brewery, the Hair of the Frog, had just opened in Grand Rapids. Kevin Holmes, the third cog in the Shawn and Don machine, took us out there one dark night, and it soon became our favorite hangout. (In fact, twelve years later, it's now The Hideout Brewing Company and still my favorite hangout.)

As we enjoyed the flavorful adult beverages throughout the winter, we learned more about the art of brewing good beer and about the little trails right out the back door of the Frog. We'd go out after work and follow the trail through the swamp and woods and a couple residential neighborhoods. Spring fever was upon us, and we were itching for another event.

The trails were still muddy from spring rains, but they provided a perfect place to stage a run with friends. The idea of another Friday night event appealed to us. Now to find a good Friday to have it. Wait, that's it! Good Friday. It was Friday the 13th, 2001, and it was time for the Frogger 5.5K.

While measuring the course, we just couldn't make it back to the brewery in only 3.1 miles/5 kilometers, no matter how we designed the route. So, it became the Frogger 5.5K, more or less. It turned out a new friend, Jake, the Frog's bartender and son of the owner, was quite an artist. Before we knew it, we had posters and a clever T-shirt design. Gazelle Sports agreed to sponsor us by providing race numbers and gift certificates.

Figuring maybe 30-40 people would show up, we were blown away when 62 entered the race. We had runners from as far away as Portage, Ludington, Lansing, and even three guys from New Zealand who happened to be in town. We ran out of numbers and shirts.

At the starting whistle, the anxious runners headed for the nature trail. "Big" John Rothwell had a plan. He knew he couldn't outrun all those ectomorphic speedy guys, but he knew he could block. Running his butt off for the first 30 yards to get a lead heading into the trail, he succeeded in keeping the rest of the pack behind him. With his size working to his advantage, nobody could get by on the trail. It wouldn't work for long, however. Another John, soon-to-be-race-winner (and ectomorphic speedy guy) John Lipa, dove through the trees and blew by the big guy (on his third attempt).

Runners followed a trail of toilet paper hanging from the trees, chalk arrows on the trail and road, and signs made by Jake and his wife, Holly, with a cute little running frog on them. Kilometer marks were on the road in chalk, since we figured that would be better than mile marks. After all, no self-respecting American has a clue what his pace per kilometer is, so we could get away with the course being short or long.

After a loop around a lake, John Lipa emerged from the trail far ahead of the pack, finishing in a blazing 20:36. Our women's winner, Amy Wing, came in at 23:38. Everybody set personal records for the distance. Only no one really knew what the distance was. We were pretty sure that runners who paid for 5.5K got more than their money's worth, though.

Big John stopped to enjoy a post-race cigarette, and we went back into the brewery for some refreshing adult beverages. Our winners and the DFL (Dead...uh...Freakin' Last) runner were rewarded with a genuine Hair of the Frog beer glass and a gift certificate from Gazelle

Sports.

The end of 2001 would bring about another Shawn and Don conspiracy, as well as my very first professional (i.e., I got paid!) article, published in *Michigan Runner* magazine.

Running Naked on the South Beltline

by Don Kern

The first section of a new bypass around the south side of Grand Rapids officially opened for vehicular traffic Wednesday, November 21. The previous Sunday, however, saw some traffic of a different kind.

A group of a dozen runners from a local running club realized it was the last chance to run on the new five-mile section of freeway known locally as the South Beltline, more formally as the Paul B. Henry Freeway (M-6). We met at eight Sunday morning in the pea-soup fog at Cascade Park southeast of Grand Rapids to begin our running odyssey. Steph positioned her van just over five miles west on Broadmoor (M-37) to shuttle the people who didn't want to do the whole out-and-back loop.

About three miles out, Big John started to laugh. "You know what would be funny as heck? Running naked on the South Beltline." Shawn rode beside us on his bike, and the Little Mexican—David—ran with us as well. We had a good laugh at the suggestion, but the next thing we knew, Big John lost the shirt and running shorts. He ran about a quarter mile, enjoying the fresh, foggy air.

Already coming back on the other side, the fast guys in the group caught a bit of John's show. Scott, the red-headed skinny guy, decided to get in on the act as well, so then we had naked guys running both sides of the road.

We ran west to Broadmoor, south, and then back up the ramp on the other side, heading east. After about a mile, just Big John and I were running together, and it occurred to me, "This is the only chance I'll ever have to run naked on the South Beltline." What the heck. I stripped down to just my running shoes and water-bottle belt. There I was, running naked down the freeway in the middle of November.

Some girls were walking just one way on the course, and, as fate would have it, we saw them off in the distance through the fog. It was, however, too late to do anything about it by that time, so we decided to run by them as quickly as possible and make the best of it. We met them just as they crossed over to the west-bound lanes.

Shawn had met the ladies a few minutes earlier and was riding along beside them. He tells the story:

"'Who are those two coming this way?' one of the ladies asked. 'Are those runners? It's hard to tell in the fog.' I said, 'Yes. From their strides, it looks like Big John on the left and Marathon Don on the right.'

"As the two figures got closer coming out of the fog, someone exclaimed, 'Are they?' 'They're not!' 'Yes, they're naked!' They came running by us with their clothes in hand and other body parts freely swaying in the wind! People shouted and applauded as the two streaked by."

"It was surreal," one woman said. "Two Greek-god-like silhouettes appearing out of the fog, totally naked." OK, that may be a slight misquote. Actually, I think somebody said, "I thought they called him BIG John?!"

After passing the girls, we put our clothes back on. Shawn made sure the girls got to the van, then headed back out on his bike to catch up with us. We were a couple miles from the end when suddenly Shawn screamed, "SHRINKAGE!!" as he blazed by on the bicycle, naked as a jaybird.

The First South Beltline Naked Run ended uneventfully, with no one getting arrested. The fog here in Grand Rapids kept us from seeing the Leonid meteor shower Sunday morning. But someone DID report seeing a FULL MOON.

The Escapades Continue

Over the next couple years, "Shawn and Don Events" went on to produce a few more off-the-wall races.

One September, taking advantage of the newly paved roads through the former Butterworth Landfill near downtown, we staged the Gate Crasher, another small event that was pretty much just a Grand Rapids Running Club excuse to party a little bit.

On Saturday night of St. Patrick's Day weekend, several of us were enjoying a post-Irish Jig 5K beer at the Hair of the Frog. The Irish Jig is one of the "rites of spring" if you're a runner in Grand Rapids. "The Little Mexican," David Castillo, came up with a flash of inspiration. (We call David "the Little Mexican" because he's little and, well, Mexican.) "They have the Irish Jig for St. Patrick's Day; why don't they have a Run for the Border for Cinco de Mayo?"

Partly cloudy brains started storming, and the next thing we knew, we had a plan. On May 5, we met at the bike bridge on Indian Mounds Road with David translating instructions to the runners in Spanish. We crammed everyone we could into the back of Shawn's van, smuggled them to the popular Mexican food joint, The Adobe Restaurant, and opened the back doors to mark the start of the run. The mission? Cross the Rio Grande. In Grand Rapids, we call it the Grand River.

There was no set course; just get there any way possible. Everyone who crossed the bridge was given a green card, after which we headed to Shawn's for cold Coronas, tacos, and a piñata. (By the way, if you're looking for political correctness, you're in the wrong book.)

"These were the quirky ideas you get when you have a pint of beer and you're quite active, so you just come up with things," Shawn said.

Three more runnings of the Frogger 5.5K gave "Shawn and Don" a bit of a cult following in the local running community. The third annual event took place during an ice storm that took out the electricity in a large part of the city later that night and earned our event a prime spot on the local Fox News affiliate, WXMI-TV, as well as a story in the editor's introduction column in *Michigan Runner* magazine.

"We had a pretty decent influence, and it grew fast," Shawn said. "It was a lot of fun."

Shawn and I were co-conspirators in a bunch of interesting runs and had a blast running our friends through creeks and cemeteries, climbing sand hills, and almost anything else we could talk people into. The more "off the wall" it was, the better we liked it. Friday evenings usually involved a run and some food and brews as we conspired with our friends about the next event. It was a great time of life.

On a Wednesday evening in the fall of 2003, yet another flash of inspiration would strike while running with the Grand Rapids Running Club.

Chapter 11

Birth of a Marathon

In mid-October 2003, while running with the Grand Rapids Running Club on one of our regular Wednesday evening runs, we took some time to venture into unexplored territory. As a part of the Millennium Park development on the southwest side of Grand Rapids, new trails were being paved through the woods along the Grand River.

We followed the trails past the popular River Boat landing at the far end of Indian Mounds Road, through the woods to the Grandville Sewer Plant and back. Foot bridges weren't in yet, but there were logs we could balance on to cross Buck Creek. Shawn and I were doing math and having discussions the whole way back to Johnson Park.

Our conclusion: "A couple 13-mile out-and-back loops, and we could just about put on a marathon here."

Game on. A week or so later, we convened a group of running

friends for another brainstorming session at the Hair of the Frog Brewery (which Shawn had purchased earlier that year) and put our collective thoughts down on paper. A bit of beer and bullsh*t later, and the event was developing rapidly. We set a date of October 31, 2004, to hold the first Grand Rapids Marathon.

A few thought that with less than a year to prepare, we were in for more than we could pull off. My reaction to anyone saying something like that (at least in my head) is generally, "Really? Stand the f*ck back and watch this."

Indeed, there were plenty of details, but any given individual task was pretty easy. The key was to commit. That part was easy. Registering a website takes five minutes. Putting the race on marathon calendars at MarathonGuide.com and *Runner's World* is another few minutes. Because MarathonGuide.com had become the place to go for information on 26.2-mile events, we used their service to do our race registration. Thoughts and plans went on through the winter, with a half-marathon option added, along with a two-person relay.

As soon as spring had sprung, our registration went live. On March 24, 2004, only a few minutes after it was even possible, Mark Sirios became the first-ever person to register for the inaugural Grand Rapids Marathon. There was no turning back now. By the end of October, another 929 people signed up to join Mark on Halloween. The race was on!

As the event took shape, people jumped on board, eager to be part of the event. People we ran with regularly grabbed the reins and made things happen. Lynne Oosterhouse wanted to handle volunteers. Kathy Haase volunteered for packet pickup. Rick Ganzi suggested during a run one morning that we should have pace teams. My first inclination was, "Why? We're going to be a fairly small marathon." But shortly after that, the good doctor came up with a flash of brilliance, proposing pace teams based on the marathon times of celebrity runners. The world's first ever "Celebrity" pace teams were thus conceived. Oprah Winfrey had the

4:29 pace, for example, while P. Diddy (or whatever he's calling himself these days) was at 4:14, Will Ferrell at 3:56, George W. Bush at 3:44 and Billy Baldwin at the very respectable – and slightly surprising – 3:29. Somehow, the times worked out to approximately every fifteen minutes.

On March 27, I paid a visit to the Martian Marathon in Northville, Michigan, and spent time with race directors Randy Step and Tami Duquette, hoping to learn from some nearby experts. The Martian Marathon is a great small race; about the size we expected our Grand Rapids event to be. Randy and Tami were full of information about handling medals, course certification, volunteers, and finish-line results.

On the second Friday of May, we had a booth at the Fifth Third River Bank Run Expo, arguably the best race in West Michigan, a 25K race held annually in downtown Grand Rapids. It was our debut event, and it made a big splash. During the morning of that expo, Mike Lapp, who owned Crystal Cleaners at the time, came up to me and pressed a couple hundred dollars into my hand. "This has gotta happen," he said, and thus became one of our first sponsors.

Several people signed up that day, and somehow WOOD TV-8, the area's local NBC affiliate, got wind of a marathon in Grand Rapids. The next day, following the River Bank Run, they caught up with me for an interview. A few people saw it, and four days later, Terence Reuben was on the phone, wanting to know how to get Metro Health Sports Medicine in as our medical team. We met for coffee a couple days later, and a great friendship was born.

Reuben and the Metro Health team had been providing medical support for the Fifth Third River Bank Run for years. He assumed we already had that kind of thing in place. We would have gotten around to it eventually, but it was nice of him to offer.

"I was expecting to walk over to Don and find out, 'We're good. We have it covered.' Hey, this is a marathon. You don't put on a marathon without having these things in place," Reuben said. "Our first meeting, we hit it off so well. Don had the passion for what we're trying to do. I could see the passion for what he wanted to do for this community, and he could see my passion for wanting to keep the community safe. That was a great start."

Soon afterward, Jeff Miles from RW Baird Investments contacted me to find out how Baird could get involved. Suddenly, from out of nowhere, we had sponsors.

Originally, we were hoping to use online registration exclusively, but even in 2004 there were people who didn't want to use the Internet or didn't trust typing in their credit card number. We threw together some fliers to accommodate those still in the analog world, put a copy on our site to download, and sent packets to running stores around the Midwest.

Early in the process, using the ability to email all of the runners from the registration site brought some great interactions. Runners actually love to be consulted about what they would like to see at our marathon, and the feedback on course support, food (I think someone recommended gummy bears and Oreo cookies), and post-race recovery was instrumental as the plans developed.

Certifying a course (i.e. making sure it's the proper distance) is critical to any marathon to make it a "Boston Qualifier," which brings many more runners than otherwise would show up. The problem, however, is that certifying a marathon would cost over $1,000, and at that time, there was no way of knowing how much it would cost to put on the race and how many would register. So I downloaded the manuals from the USA Track & Field web site, bought a Jones-Oerth Counter for my bike, and learned how to measure courses for certification.

Most everything that year was done very conservatively. Staging at Millennium Park, staying off all the main roads, and using the same course twice cut out a lot of costs we otherwise might have spent on police and traffic control, which helped keep our expenses to a minimum. It also made working with municipalities very easy, the whole venture taking only a couple of meetings with cops and park officials.

That summer brought some transitions in the team. Shawn had some business and family priorities to take care of, so he left Grand Rapids for a few months for a job in South Carolina, leaving me to organize the marathon. Changes in my marital situation had me living at Shawn's house while he worked in the sunny South.

Only one price increase was scheduled for our race fees, set to happen on August 15. As that day approached, online registrations peaked, and an envelope arrived in the mail filled with twenty registrations from runners at a local company. Suddenly it was clear: We can afford to do this thing.

The park staff at Millennium Park wanted to cap our numbers at 500 runners. After agreeing to run shuttle busses from some nearby parking lots, we negotiated that number up to 750. Beyond that, estimating that 10-percent of registrants might not show up, we continued to take more runners as we topped the 750 mark. (And no, I didn't tell the staff at Millennium we went over our quota.) Somewhere around October 10, we cut off online registration, having reached our limit. However, saying "No" was never my strong suit, so when someone made a good case to get in, the response was usually, "Okay, but it will cost you a beer." I received a clever email from Gary VanDyken titled "Top 10 Reasons My Wife Sandy Should Be Allowed to Run the Half Marathon," and replied with the normal response.

As I worked in my normal coffee shop one morning, Gary came in with an application in his hand for his wife, Sandy. He walked up, handed me the application, and set a can of Sam Adams down on the table where I was working. "This is nice," I thought out loud and had another flash of inspiration. On the website's "Race Day Instruction" page, I added another item: *Beer – Bring a bottle of decent beer as a gift for the race director.* Good move! Thus began a tradition that continues to this day.

A couple weeks before our first race, I ran the Run Thru Apple

Country 10K. During the race, some of the runners around me were talking about the marathon.

"It scares the heck out of me," I said.

"Are you running it?"

"No. I'm the race director."

It was the biggest project of my life, and there were no options but to make sure it happened when and where it was supposed to happen. There were tons of details, but between the sponsors and a great staff, lots of good people were helping with the event.

Since we had a staff that included many marathon runners who would be awfully busy on race weekend, we decided to hold a "dress rehearsal" on Sunday, October 24, a week before our event, so we could earn our medals. Mike Lapp, who was not only a sponsor but had joined the staff, decided to also have the distinction of being the first official finisher of the event. He started somewhere around 2 a.m. and ran the whole course, *naked except for his running shoes.* As we arrived to start the staff run that Sunday morning, the earliest of us caught the end of Mike's marathon.

Race weekend came, and we held a small expo and packet pickup at Kosciuszko Hall, one of the Polish Catholic halls on the West Side of Grand Rapids where Shawn and I had been hanging out in recent months. (Though neither of us are Polish or Catholic.) Alan Martens, owner of the running specialty store Running Circles, and Metro Health Sports Medicine were our only vendors. Kosciuszko Hall staff provided the traditional pre-marathon pasta dinner.

On Saturday, the day before our race, the wind was so strong our port-a-johns blew over. We scrambled to round up as much hose as we could to rinse out the blue stuff that had sloshed all over everything (fortunately, there was no "brown stuff" in any of them yet) and lined them up back to back in the hope that they wouldn't blow over again. Mike Lapp went out with his crew later that night to set up the medical tent, a "portable garage" we had bought for the occasion. Unfortunately, the wind hadn't died down yet, and the medical tent Mike and company were setting up blew into the lake in the middle of the night.

The wind calmed a little bit for Sunday, but not as much as we would have liked. At 3 a.m., Francine and I were stringing tarps along the sides of the pavilion at Millennium Park to make an enclosed place out of the wind for runners to pick up their race bibs.

"I just remember not knowing what to expect," Francine said. "We were as prepared as we could have been, probably more than most first-time marathons, but things happened that we didn't plan for. The mile markers weren't up. We had planned on volunteers doing that, but Nancy Scheer and I had to hop in a van and race against the clock to get the mile markers out before the race started. When it all came together and was all done and the last person had gone home, it was like, 'Wow, we did this.'"

As 5 a.m. approached, I was standing on a ladder at the pavilion, hanging a sign and surveying the landscape. *I have no idea how we can be ready before the 7 a.m. "Velocity Challenged" start.* Then something magical happened. People started showing up. Jeanne Wilcox, who was coordinating the medical logistics, arrived at a time when the medical tent fiasco was in its full glory. When I saw her, it suddenly hit me. *I have someone in charge of that!* I grabbed her and kissed her right on the forehead. Somehow, Dr. Ed Kornoelje, Terence Reuben, and their small team figured out how to set up a makeshift medical unit using the pieces and parts left of the medical tent that blew away.

Reuben remembers thinking everything was running like clockwork—until he actually arrived the morning of the race. Once he navigated through the long line of cars trying to enter Millennium Park, he helped piece together the medical tent, finishing about ten minutes before the race started. He left Dr. Ed Kornoelje in charge of the tent and went out to run his first half-marathon.

"There were a bunch of pipes and poles and pieces of top lying around, but no tent. We got the poles up, grabbed some duct tape, and made a M*A*S*H unit out of it," Reuben said. "It was a little chaotic to say the least. But that first year taught us so much about what we were truly capable of doing and handling. Everything just grew from that. In retrospect, it was great. On the day of? Yeah, it was crazy."

Timers from Gault Race Management arrived and set up their chip-reading mats and time clocks. TJ the DJ brought the sound system and started kicking out the music. He took one look at me as he was setting up and said, "Jeez, dude, you need a Red Bull?"

TJ the DJ is otherwise known as TJ Suchocki, who has owned and operated TJ the DJ Entertainment since before he was 18 years old. TJ's dry cleaner, none other than Mike Lapp, first introduced us. He was hesitant to take the marathon gig initially because he would be DJing the night before until 3 a.m., then would have to break down his equipment and set it back up before the runners started filing into the park.

His initial survey of the scene may not have calmed his concerns.

"The weather was absolutely terrible, but I took one look at him, because they had been tipping up the port-o-potties from the wind and cleaning them out, and was like, 'You need a Red Bull, man? You Okay?'" Suchocki said. "That was my first experience. I also was like, this guy is freaking nuts. Are you kidding me?"

The rest of the staff arrived, and while it might not be called a well-oiled machine, the passion of the crew was obvious as we prepared for the start. Francine and Nancy left with the mile markers and barely stayed ahead of the runners but got them all in place on time. At 7 a.m., the early start went off, and over the next hour, the shuttle busses were bringing runners in from a couple remote lots where we had arranged overflow parking. Things were happening! At about 7:50 it became apparent that all the runners wouldn't be shuttled in from the remote parking lots before the scheduled 8 a.m. start time, so my mom's favorite race director made an executive decision to delay the start for twenty minutes to make sure everyone got to the starting line. Surprisingly, everyone seemed to take it in stride and understood the need for the delay.

At 8:20 a.m., in what I still identify as the most relieved moment of my life, the starting gun went off. The realization of an amazing goal was underway, and with a lump in my throat, I watched for the next two or three minutes as runners filed past me, starting their 26.2-mile journey. The event we spent months planning had become a reality.

The weather was a mixture of everything imaginable, with wind, rain, sleet, snow, and sunshine as the day went on. Some of the runners went off in costume in honor of Halloween. Many were losing their marathon virginity, taking advantage of a hometown marathon for a life changing experience.

Two hours and thirty-four minutes later, Erik Bush cruised in, stopping a few yards short to pick up his kids and carry them across the finish line, winning the first Grand Rapids Marathon. A few minutes later at 2:58, Debra Gormley of St. Paul, Minnesota, won the women's race. Somewhere around 3:30 p.m., the final finisher crossed the line. Our race was a success!

Some runner comments:

My hat's off to you and your team for putting on a great event. The magnitude of such an undertaking and the effort that must go into planning and executing something like this is truly amazing. And when one thinks of trying to please nearly 1,000 runners with all their odd mannerisms, expectations and personality traits, it makes me question your sanity. But you did it! And, you did it well!!

The course, volunteers, water stations, start/finish areas and logistics were excellent. The hotel arrangements (and even the weather) were great. And the post-race party at the hall was a nice added touch (for me and the other three people that I met there). I've already recommended next year's event to other runners and will continue to do so.

Congratulations and thanks for a great time.

-Kevin Galvin; Plymouth, Michigan

Don-

This was my fifth marathon and you guys/gals did a GREAT job. Great course, well organized and well managed. Thanks for your tremendous work.

-Chris Womack

Don,

I would like to take the opportunity to thank you and the support group for putting on a very good marathon. I have run some 30 marathons and this was as professional as anyone could expect for a first year marathon. I am sure that there was lots of learning. But all in all, it was a great event. I am already looking forward to next year's race. I am sure that this race will be one of the best in the Midwest.

I will keep this short; I just felt compelled to express my gratitude for a very good marathon.

Thank You!

Gene McClain

The staff, by that time feeling pretty worn out, stayed around to finish cleaning up. By around 5 p.m., the runners had gone home, the mess was cleaned up, and a couple park-employee kids were busted for sneaking beer out of our keg while we weren't looking.

We were running out of steam, but before sunset. it was hardly evident that we had been at Millennium Park. It was time for a well-deserved beer to celebrate. We had a loosely planned after-party back at Kosciuszko Hall.

Most party-goers had gone home by the time the few of us from the staff arrived. Several, however, were still enjoying the rehydration process. My eyes got moist in a hurry when the few who remained rose to their feet and gave me a standing ovation.

Grand Rapids has a marathon!

Chapter 12

Grand Rapids Has a Marathon!

The first Grand Rapids Marathon was in the books, and on the following Tuesday, the next big race was scheduled—between George W. Bush and John Kerry for the presidency of the United States. The early edition of Monday's *Grand Rapids Press* had this headline plastered on the front page:

BUSH PRESIDES OVER INAUGURAL GR MARATHON

Editors were quick on their feet, though, and before the later edition came out, the headline was changed to read:

THIS BUSH PRESIDES OVER INAUGURAL GR MARATHON

While our former president did have a pretty respectable marathon time at one point, even becoming the inspiration for one of our pace teams, my friend and fellow member of the worldwide online running club, the Dead Runners Society, Erik Bush of Warrenville, Illinois, who prevailed in 2:34:11. He ran the final stretch holding the hand of his 4-year-old son. One marathon down and one course record established. Oh, that other Bush? He won, too.

That first marathon set more than simply a time precedent, of course.

Paving the Way

The West Michigan area wasn't a stranger to marathons before this event was founded. The Grand Valley Marathon organized by the Y's Men (now known as the YMCA Service Club) in the early 1970s has continued annually, and in 2012, it celebrated its 43rd running. The distances shortened over the years and the name changed, but the same organization still organizes what has become the oldest race in Michigan. It became the Run Thru Apple Country 5K and 10K until just a few years ago.

In 2005, when the venue moved to the brand new David D. Hunting YMCA in downtown Grand Rapids, the name was changed again to the Run Thru The Rapids. In 2011, the Run Thru The Rapids became part of the marathon weekend, rounding out a series of events that now includes a marathon, half-marathon, marathon relay, kids marathon, health and fitness expo, and a 5K and 10K. The Greater Grand Rapids Marathon was held for two years in the late 1980s, but dissolved after its short run due to lack of participation and money, according to The Grand Rapids Press archives.

As the years rolled by and the Grand Rapids Marathon blossomed, the event had plenty of notable moments and traditions.

Beer

Among the traditions and precedents set at our first marathon was one near and dear to my heart. When Gary VanDyken responded f(l)avorably to my suggestion that entering his wife, Sandy, into the half marathon would cost him a beer, it prompted another idea.

On the race day instructions page of the website, I semi-jokingly suggested that participants could bring a decent bottle of beer as a gift for the race director. That fateful Halloween morning, before the first runner crossed the starting line, "TJ the DJ" handed me a big can of Foster's and said, "Someone left this here for you." Before the day ended, my beer collection had grown somewhere north of 50. It's a tradition that prevails to this day, and guests at my house are sure to find something interesting in the beer fridge.

Love

Our first romance blossomed during that inaugural weekend. Bill and Amy Elvey met at our first marathon and now are not only married, they are also lifetime entrants to the Grand Rapids Marathon.

That wasn't our only love story.

In 2005, Ted Watkins sought me out during the race expo to ask for my permission to propose to Colleen Brown at the finish line. It was like being the father of the bride. Of course, I said "yes." So did she. The next year, she ran as Colleen Watkins.

In 2011, Che Morris posted on Facebook her intention to marry Steve Strasser during the marathon "if she could convince her favorite Race Director . . . " That was an easy sale. The Austin, Texas, couple started the morning at Millennium Park, the site of our first marathon, got hitched, and then ran a bit over a half-marathon. They finished the race as husband and wife, stopping to dance at the aid stations. The bride wore a wedding dress made of white, sweat-wicking fabric.

Downtown

For the second running, in October 2005, we moved the start and finish line to downtown Grand Rapids after the $30 million David D. Hunting YMCA opened on July 5, 2005. We outgrew Millennium Park our first year, and the new Y proved the ideal venue. We held a real expo in a pair of exercise studios on the second floor, and the building offered runners a place to stay warm before the race and shower afterward.

The first version of our downtown course headed straight out of town, taking advantage of a fairly new and as yet unused road through the former Butterworth Landfill site. We headed out Butterworth road and then took advantage of Millennium Park and Indian Mounds Road. As Millennium Park has developed, we've enjoyed using more of the wide paved trails, making the course even more desirable as the years go by.

Pickle Juice

It was at our second running in 2005 when we first served pickle juice on the course, a move inspired by Dr. Rick Ganzi. You'll remember Rick as our Pace Team Director and was the instigator of the celebrity pace teams. He first started drinking the salty brine to ward off cramps during the 2001 Detroit Marathon, and we subsequently became the first marathon to serve pickle juice to its participants. Since then, we've been featured for that accomplishment—if that's the right word—on at least three continents.

The pickle juice culture spread through the years. In 2011, participant Jill Plamondone mailed this to me: "I have looked for easy carry pouches and found PicklePops out of TX which is actually crushed pickles in the juice. During the GR Marathon last year, I found myself craving it the entire race after the swig at mile 17. It was amazing how fast it worked and gave me some spring in my step. My run buddy is now also a believer after we used it in the Bayshore marathon (in Traverse City, Michigan). I used it again in a half and she didn't have any and muttered, 'Oh great, now I have to keep up with the power of the pickle.' Power to the pickle."

Celebrity Involvement

In 2006, my good friend and ultramarathoner Dean Karnazes was running 50 marathons in 50 states in 50 consecutive days and chose Grand Rapids for his Michigan event. As a result, our dress rehearsal for the Grand Rapids Marathon was moved to a Saturday so Dean and company could join us. We were state No. 35 on his quest, and were joined by David Willey, the editor of *Runner's World* magazine, as well as about 100 more runners from around the country—and it wasn't even our race day.

When the actual race rolled around the next weekend, Jimi Minnema, an excellent athlete from nearby Jenison, won in 2:39:34, making him the first locally-based runner to capture the event.

The 2007 Grand Rapids Marathon owes a debt (sort of) to the Chicago Marathon. A few weeks earlier, temperatures in the Windy City soared into the 90s. I was pacing at that event, and as we approached mile 19 at approximately 11:30 a.m., the race was halted for the first time in its 30-year history. Unseasonable 95-degree heat resulted in hundreds of runners falling ill and many others dropping out. After finishing the course despite the cancellation, I spent the drive home strategizing how we could take advantage of the situation, and get some of the disappointed runners into our race that would take place three weeks later.

As it turned out, strategy was unnecessary. When I got home, my email was lit up with 50 more registrations from people who wanted to take advantage of their hard work and training after they were kicked off the Chicago course. The next morning, I called my Maxwell Medals sales guy, Michael Foster, and arranged for a couple hundred more finisher medals. Thankfully, our sponsors stepped up and helped with additional food, water, and Gatorade. We saw nearly a 40-percent growth that year.

That was good news for Metro Health, which had upgraded its involvement to title sponsor. In 2007, it became the Metro Health

Grand Rapids Marathon. We also added a kids marathon, with youngsters training for 25 miles beginning in early August and then running their last 1.2 miles on the course the day before the marathon. Nearly 1,000 children participate in our kids event every year.

At the pasta dinner in 2007, Chuck Engle, who holds the world record for most marathon wins as of 2012, came up to me and asked about the course record. It was 2:32:47, held by Erik Bush, who had defended his 2004 title in 2005.

"It's going down" was Engle's reply. The next day, Chuck made good on his promise and became our course record holder, in 2:31:47.

The "Lifetime Runner" idea was born in 2008 in a conversation with a friend, Dan Manning, in a bar after a Grand Rapids Griffins minor league hockey game. The ideas were flying back and forth when inspiration hit. To this date, it still appears we're the only race offering a lifetime entry fee option.

Babies and Canadians

One day in 2009, my phone rang with a rather bewildered call from the obstetrics ward at Metro Health Hospital. A woman there had a baby and wanted to know how to redeem her coupon for a free entry to the marathon in October. That was in response to a coupon in my regular newsletter, which offered a free entry to anyone having a baby at Metro Health. Through 2012, we've had over a dozen babies.

That same year, I noticed that the town of London, Ontario, had nearly as many runners registered as the entire state of Indiana. So I laid down a challenge: If Ontario could beat Indiana, I would sing the Canadian national anthem. Little did I know they had organized two buses to transport more than a hundred runners to the starting line. I'd like to think my rendition of "O Canada" still resonates with those participants.

The Success Continues

We had our first Olympic trials qualifier in 2010, after former University of Michigan standout Katie Jazwinski won the women's title with a time of 2:44:59. Through 22 miles, she actually led the entire race and still managed to finish fifth overall. Her time also shattered the women's record by more than thirteen minutes.

The World's Most Amazing Marathon Staff

When an event is organized by a group of people who love running, it's bound to be a positive influence. That's exactly what happens here, with a staff of runners who collectively have over 600 marathons worth of experience. Many have been on the staff since the first year. Even as our event has grown from around 900 runners in 2004 to a whole weekend involving over 6,000 runners and volunteers, the staff still do an even better job every year.

"I knew that it would be successful and keep going, and I'm not surprised by that, but I really like to see what's happened," Francine said. "It's become a well-oiled machine. Everybody is passionate about what they're doing, and everybody works so well together. It's not just a running event anymore. It's a community event."

Pass It On

The opportunity to share the experience with others presented itself unexpectedly on a cold winter day in 2010.

The Fox Valley Marathon in St. Charles, Illinois, was a dream that started when race directors Dave Sheble and Craig Bixler ran in the 2007 Grand Rapids Marathon after the infamously hot Chicago Marathon. Dave says he shook my hand at the finish line. He left inspired by the personal touches I've strived to include in the event. In January 2010, he called me out of the blue. "Can I ask you a few questions? We figure you're the ultimate resource." An hour and a half later, we hung up.

Dave still has the original, hand-written page of notes he took when we had our first phone call.

"It could have been perceived as competition for him, or he could have said, 'It's taken me a long time to develop this formula and all these ins and outs, and I had to learn it on my own, and you should, too,' but it was exactly the opposite," Sheble said. "We framed out what we thought was a good way to start, but there were so many details and directions to go, and he was more than willing, gushing with information and asking questions and really took a personal interest in helping us out. It's pretty obvious now, years later, that he's done this for a number of people."

I did my best to help out with specifics like sponsorships, course layouts, hydration stations, medical needs, and marketing. That fall in September 2010, Dave and Craig staged the first Fox Valley Marathon in the suburbs along the Fox River west of Chicago. Francine and I do our best to visit the event every year, just as the Fox Valley staff does in Grand Rapids.

The Fox Valley Marathon debuted in 2010 with 1,100 runners. In 2012, numbers had grown to nearly 2,800 competing in the marathon, half-marathon, and a 20-mile event.

"Any time we talk, we'll usually go back to 'How are things going? What are you doing?'" Sheble said. "But we also have become really good friends. It's just evolved into a very good friendship. There are countless numbers of mes out there Don has helped and influenced. I'm just one in a line."

Back home in Grand Rapids, Fred Bunn, who was the director of the East Grand Rapids Parks and Recreation Department and has been an influential figure in the running community throughout West Michigan, told The *Grand Rapids Press* back in 2004 he was happy to see a marathon return to the area.

"Is it a good thing? Absolutely it is," he told the newspaper. "The running community in the Grand Rapids area all the way out to the lakeshore offers top road runs at every distance but the marathon. I would hope that with Millennium Park and holding the race in the fall, it will attract both Grand Rapids area, state, and regional athletes."

Chuck Engle, our 2007 winner, has long been another fan of the race, emailing me following one race: "I try to analyze the races for something that I can let the race director work on for the next race. Yours was the first marathon that I have thought about, and I am unable to offer any discernible critique to help."

Since 2004, more than 20-percent of Grand Rapids Marathon runners have qualified for the Boston Marathon, one of ten races with the largest percentage of qualifiers, according to Active.com. RunningUSA.org reported in its 2011 annual report that Grand Rapids had the fifth-fastest median time in the country at 3:59:33.

Julie Deardorff also published this in her blog at the *Chicago Tribune*'s website in April 2007: "Yes, this is a serious marathon. Certified distance, chip timed, Boston qualifier, USATF sanctioned. The race director, however, is a little less serious. 'Smart, good-looking, and dedicated, but not serious.' . . . It's also logistically easier than a mega marathon: easier to get where you want to go, easier to navigate to manage the bag drop offs, easier to find your friends and family at the finish."

TJ Suchocki, the only DJ the Grand Rapids Marathon has ever had, seems to enjoy staying around with me waiting for the last finishers, in spite of what he says: "Don is such a cool guy, and it pisses me off every year, but he wants to wait until the last person finishes so everyone gets the same experience. To have somebody in charge of an event like this who commits to every single person, you just don't get that. That's not the world we live in."

"As race director of the Grand Rapids Marathon, Don encourages and motivates everyone to set goals, work towards them, and be successful," said Brent Weigner. "Don is not built like a marathoner. Some people don't even consider him a serious athlete. Because of those very facts, people look at him and listen to him and think, 'Hey, if he can achieve those things, I can certainly run a marathon.' I think he inspires ordinary people who would never think of running a marathon."

Over the past decade, runners of all shapes, sizes, and velocities have crossed our finish line, doing something they never thought possible.

Lives have changed as runners worked toward the incredible goal of running 26.2 miles. I've been fortunate to greet thousands of them at the finish line, witnessing that incredible moment with them. It's one of the most magical places on the planet, the end of a long journey, the accomplishment of a massive goal. Emotions run high, and the mixture of joy, pain, and success is nearly overwhelming. Sharing that moment with runners is a powerful experience. Never do I get through a day at the finish line without a tear or two rolling down my cheek as I share those moments.

We've been able to contribute tens of thousands of dollars to charities as well. Alternatives in Motion, a local charity that provides power wheelchairs to those who can't otherwise get them, has been a partner for many years now. The YMCA Strong Kids Campaign is another of our favorite causes. We also contribute to charities that run aid stations or help us out in numerous ways. Sharing and giving back were some of the reasons for starting the marathon back in 2004.

At this writing, the 2012 Grand Rapids Marathon had been completed on another beautiful October afternoon, and plans are underway for the 10th annual event in 2013. On February 2, 2013, our new Groundhog Day Marathon made its debut on a 4.4-mile course that was repeated six times, reminiscent of the 1993 movie *Groundhog Day* that starred Bill Murray.

All the while the hometown marathon was growing, there was still some unfinished business. Two world record attempts in 2007 followed by knee problems and a slower-than-hoped-for recovery was a little discouraging, but I was starting to feel better. Richard Donovan's Antarctic Ice Marathon would be the key to making it happen. Then again, Richard always seemed to lure me into running in the most inhospitable places on the planet. Take 2003, for example . . .

Chapter 13

The North Pole Marathon

The huge Russian came at my nose with a fist almost as big as my head. Resistance was futile. Besides, it was for my own good. There was a lot of love in those big hands.

The 2002 South Pole Marathon expedition left a bit of rivalry between Richard Donovan and Dean Karnazes, with both having completed a marathon at the South Pole and looking to make it a matched set. Richard was the first to make it a reality, when in March 2002, he went on an expedition to the North Pole, running laps around a helicopter in sub-sub-zero conditions. Doing so, he became the first person to ever cover the marathon distance at the Earth's northernmost point. His solo North Pole run turned out to be a scouting mission, and soon afterward, he formulated a plan to organize the North Pole Marathon. If you've read this far, you know what would happen as soon as I got wind of it. And you're right.

Spending as many enjoyable days and nights together as Richard, Brent Weigner, and I had during the South Pole adventure made us, by my definition, friends forever. We had endured hardships, woken up in the same places, overcome adversities, and come home with common stories. Those kind of things join people together in a way few other things can.

After spending nearly the whole month of January 2002 together in the Antarctic, the three of us would reunite for the first North Pole Marathon. This event propelled Richard into the race director business. Soon, he would establish another Antarctic marathon, taking place in the Patriot Hills. He now directs both the northernmost and southernmost marathons on earth, making it possible for people like you and me to enjoy some pretty awesome adventures. Some other recurring characters you've already met in these pages joined us: Paul Ruesch, Marcus Fillinger, Nelsen Petersen, Mary Ritz, and Hans VanHeerden.

The trip was historic, at least in the respect that it was the first time anyone had ever attempted such an event. Definitely worthy of a life list that includes "Visit the North Pole." My log of the expedition follows.

North Pole Marathon Log, 2003

The North Pole—the first marathon ever to be run in the middle of a frozen ocean. Brent Weigner and Richard Donovan were the co-race directors and had hooked up with Global Expeditions to make the event happen. In 2002, Richard traveled with the Russians to the pole to run a solo marathon distance as part of his own seven-continent ultra-marathon year. After spending all of January 2002 in the Antarctic with these guys, how could I turn down this adventure?

Nelsen Petersen of Kibo Productions would join us and film the adventures. Several of us would arrive in Oslo within a few days to meet for some pre-marathon fun and fellowship.

"Bring me back a rock from the North Pole," my sister Lauraine told me before I left.

"It's in the middle of a freakin' ocean," I replied. "Where are you hoping I'll find a rock?"

April 10, 2003, Grand Rapids, Michigan: The preparation process for this trip was much easier than it was for the South Pole. I owned all the gear for the trip and had experience living and running in extreme cold environments. To top that off, the winter in Michigan had been especially accommodating, with nearly every weekend from January to March in the range of 0 to 10 degrees Fahrenheit and windy. A couple extra days were added onto the first leg of the trip so I could spend the weekend at my brother-in-law Bob Portice's house near Oslo and be a tourist.

April 11: Oslo had built a new, very spacious airport since my last visit in 1996. The Flytog (express train) was a quick trip to Sandvika station, and the local bus service took me the last five kilometers to Bob's house. One of my three pretty nieces met me at the door.

April 12: I had never met Dave Kanners, a fellow Michigander and hot rod car racer from the Detroit area, but we had talked a week earlier and arranged to meet at the fountain in front of the National Theatre Underground station. Despite being in the middle of the biggest city in Norway and the fact that the fountain was dry, we had no problem finding each other. Just in case though, Dave wore his Detroit Tigers baseball cap, a universal sign that says, "I'm from Michigan." (Genetically, most everyone born in Michigan is a Tigers fan.)

Dave had been in Oslo for three days already and had seen all the sites on his "A-list," so we spent most of the morning drinking coffee, getting acquainted, and walking around town. His "B-list" included the National Gallery, a place I visited on a previous trip and was anxious to see again, so we spent the rest of the morning viewing works by famous artists such as Van Gogh, Munch, Rubens, El Greco and many others.

Dave managed to find a couple things he wouldn't mind displaying in his living room, though his appreciation for art lies more in the area of classic cars.

By lunchtime, it was, of course, time to try some local beers. After a light lunch, Dave headed off to run a few miles, and I went to do some research related to the local brewery situation. A nice bartender at the Kilkinny Inn hooked me up, and I was off to the only microbrewery in Oslo, the Oslo Mikrobryggeri.

April 13: Mary Ritz, another seven-continents runner from Cody, Wyoming, arrived in town the previous night and met Dave and me at the dry fountain. Since Dave had seen all the sights Mary wanted to see that morning, he went off in other directions, and Mary and I visited a few local museums. It was the first time I'd seen Mary since the Bozeman, Montana, marathon the previous September.

We arrived early before the museums opened and spent some time taking pictures and wandering around the grounds. An old man "adopted" us and gave us a little history lesson, which turned out to be a bit of a sales pitch, because before we knew it, we had walked with him onto his small cruise ship about to embark on a trip to Denmark. It took us a few minutes to convince him we really didn't have time to go to Denmark.

The KonTiki museum opened first, so we enjoyed a lesson on the papyrus reed boats that Thor Heyerdahl actually sailed across the ocean. Our main objective was next: the Fram Museum. The Fram is a 127-foot long schooner on which Roald Amundsen sailed south in 1911, en route to being the first man to reach the South Pole. The museum is literally built around that ship. It had the distinction of being the ship that sailed the farthest north as well as the farthest south, having been frozen into the Arctic Ocean ice and traversing the Arctic with the ice floe between 1893 and 1896. The famous telegram Amundsen sent to Captain Robert Scott (the second to reach the South Pole) is displayed: "Beg leave to inform you Fram proceeding Antarctic."

"It was so amazing to see and walk on that boat," Mary said. "I remember what a great time Don and I had being tourists and seeing all those boats that I had only read about, and now I actually saw them."

Vikingskipshuset, the Viking Ship Museum, was our next stop, for a dose of Norwegian history and heritage before returning downtown to meet Dave after lunch.

At 3 p.m., the three of us met and headed to Brent and Nelson's hotel to leave them a note with our itinerary. The next stop was The Peoples Park, home of a very famous and unusual sculpture exhibit. Sculptor Gustav Vigeland somehow talked the city fathers in Oslo into giving him a studio and money to live on in exchange for donating all his work to the city. The result was a beautiful 80-acre park filled with 192 sculptures, containing over 600 figures of naked (family-friendly, however) people. The only clothed figure in the park is a statue of Vigeland himself, with pigeon droppings all over it.

Looking at naked statues for an hour was sufficient to work up quite a thirst, so on the way back to the center of town, we stopped at the Oslo Microbrewery. Partway through our second beer, Nelsen showed up, so we had to stay for another one (darn it). We went back to pick up Brent, who couldn't get the hot water to work in the hotel and was still standing around in his underwear trying to figure it out. We talked him into putting some pants on and went out to Peppes Pizza for, well, pizza.

April 14: Monday. It's a travel day, heading north of the Arctic Circle, through Tromso, then farther north to the Svalbard Islands, an archipelago located midway between Norway and the North Pole. Spitsbergen Island is one of the largest islands and the location of the city of Longyearbyen. At the airport in Longyearbyen, our group was nearly complete—only my good friend Paul Ruesch wasn't there yet.

The bus took us all into town, and after dropping most people at the more expensive accommodations, Brent, Mary, Dave, and I were deposited at the 102 guesthouse. We unpacked in our two close-quartered rooms, then went for a short run (about 1.6 miles) to the

Radisson where most of the others were staying. There we had a small reunion (and a beer or two) with Richard Donovan. We finished our run back to the 102, cleaned up, and then walked back to the Radisson for a long get-acquainted session with the whole group at Puben (pub) at 78 North. It was there we met Curtis Lieber, the main guide on this excursion. He was soft-spoken and seemed very concerned about the welfare of everyone on the trip, as well as the people he left back home. He shared some of his philosophy: "I'm here to enjoy life and not create negative karma."

Russian Andrey Chirkov was drunk when he agreed to do his first marathon at 52 years of age. Some Englishman was going to do it, so he said he'd do one too. He spent 100 days preparing for his first marathon. Now he was 64 and up to number 75. By the way, the Englishman never showed up. Andrey's cheerful demeanor made us take to him instantly.

Helmut Linzbichler from Austria spent his winters in Michigan, working as a ski instructor at Boyne Highlands. Jovial, tough, and up for most anything, he definitely added color to the group. Dave and I claimed him as a fellow Michigander.

April 15: Standard Norwegian fare for breakfast was bread, thinly sliced ham, cheese, jam, and any other kind of sandwich filling Americans wouldn't even think of. We enjoyed a leisurely morning in the breakfast room with four girls from France, a couple Germans, a few Norwegians, and an English couple, all hearty adventure lovers in Longyearbyen for the Easter holidays.

Our digs were relatively inexpensive with comfortable small rooms as well as showers and toilets down the hall. The day's schedule was quite relaxed, so after breakfast, we spent most of the morning drinking coffee in the TV room swapping stories of our many exploits. Conversations were fascinating, and with every new story shared, my life list grew just a little bit more.

Mary and I went through town to do a bit of shopping before meeting the group for a tour of Longyearbyen. Guides, on any part of the tour that took us outside, carried guns, just in case a white bear made an appearance. After the tour, it was back for a dinner at the Radisson.

"There's a bit of whale for you," our waiter said as he left our appetizer. Not bad with a bit of salt, but I'm not sure I'd eat it all the time. Our main course was reindeer meat.

"I wonder what animal had to die for our dessert," I wondered out loud.

"Not a possum, I hope," Mary replied.

We sat by the window and watched the sun move clockwise through the sky, changing the shadows in the distant mountains, reflecting colors in the clouds. The coming Saturday would be the first night of midnight sun in Longyearbyen. This night, it would dip just below the horizon for a few minutes.

The standard pre-trip briefing followed. Our marathon group was only a subset of the North Pole adventurers, which also included a group of pole-bagger Australians with over-indulged children, some skiers out to ski the last degree to the North Pole, and a former Royal Australian Air Force photographer, diver, and mountain climber named Marcus Fillinger.

Our guide, Curtis, reminded us of the obvious necessities—boots, parka, hat, etc. We learned at this point that most of the other gear we packed would be unnecessary, as the Russians who set up the camp would provide cots, sleeping bags, heated tents, eating utensils, and nearly everything else we would need.

The tectonic movements of polar ice are very dynamic, and with the full moon on the 17th, we could expect a great deal of shifting. In fact, the runway at the camp had to be moved about seven kilometers away due to leads (cracks in the ice) opening up around the camp.

Richard and Brent held a private briefing for the marathon runners, sharing their experience of running in the extreme cold, describing the layers we would need to wear to allow us to be "comfortable" during the event. In this context, "comfortable" meant, well, something short of freezing to death.

Dark beers from the Mack Brewery, the world's northernmost, were flowing at the Puben as we got better acquainted. Getting acquainted can sometimes be a long and arduous process. Fortunately, just the right venue had presented itself.

Around midnight, we arrived back at our room and spent an hour packing and repacking for the trip north. With much of the gear checked at the inn before our team headed north, bags would be substantially lighter than planned.

April 16: At 12:45 p.m., we stood outside the 102 waiting for the bus to come get us. The wind was whipping around us until finally at 1:40, the bus arrived to take us to the Radisson in time to wait another forty-five minutes while the other travelers were accumulated. Next, we were off to the airport for another three-hour wait.

Paul Ruesch had arrived on the noon flight, so our complement of runners was complete. All it had taken to convince him to participate was a simple email.

"When I saw the email from Don with a subject line, 'Want to have some fun?', I thought *Damn!*" he said. "I didn't even open it for a week because I knew he was getting me into something again."

Paul and I have some history. He had received similar emails about Caracas and Mount Kilimanjaro. He was always a sucker for adventures. Still is.

One of his fondest memories is running the Millennium Marathon in New Zealand in 2000. The race started at 6 a.m. on New Year's Day, and the shuttles would take us to the starting line at 4 a.m., but that didn't stop us from ringing in the New Year right.

"We ended up with a rather rambunctious crowd with an affinity toward Guinness and Tillamore Dew shots, and the next thing you know, we were laughing our way back to the room just in time to hear the phone ringing, get dressed, and make the shuttle," Paul said. "I thought at the time this might be a problem since we were pretty drunk and had stayed out all night, but Don wasn't worried at all—almost as if he'd done this before. We ended up having a great run, and most of the 15 or so spectators we saw during that rainy morning were either drunk or hung over as well, so we fit right in."

After lots of delays and negotiations, the airplane's load was readjusted due to the high winds at Barneo. Unfortunately, Paul got left behind, along with one of our guides and a doctor who happened to be on the trip who had volunteered to be our medical support. Supposedly, it was a one and a half-hour flight, so in only a little over three hours, the plane would return and take the rest of the group north. (Note to readers: Never believe this kind of story.)

At 5:30, our Russian Antonov 74 lifted off for the trip north to Ice Station Barneo. Engines positioned above the wings on the Antonov 74 helped keep them from sucking in snow during landings and takeoffs. With nicely finished restrooms, a flight attendant, and seatbelts, it was almost like a regular commercial flight, if it weren't for Brent and Curtis sitting in the front row goofing around with an unloaded rifle. A somewhat humorless crew member soon took it away from them. No danger of white bears around here.

By 7 p.m., we were looking out the window at the semi-frozen Arctic Ocean. Open water divided the ice floes into a huge mosaic of irregular white tiles for as far as the eye could see. At 8:15, we landed at the new airstrip. The next half-hour was spent unloading the plane, moving all the gear to a helicopter, and reloading the plane with cargo to be sent back south. The amount of cargo the helicopter held was astounding, and when we were all loaded, the thirty or so of us piled into the same chopper, many of us on top of the gear. Rotors roared as the helicopter lifted us into the air for the final seven kilometers to the camp, dubbed Ice Station Barneo by its French and Russian crew.

The helicopter landed about 150 meters from camp, where we loaded gear onto sleds to be hauled behind snowmobiles to our tents.

We jumped over a small lead and soon came to another, about 3 feet wide, into which crew members frantically shoveled snow to form a bridge for us to cross. Dave walked backwards, taking pictures of his companions as we walked toward camp. Someone yelled at him to turn around just before he would have walked into an 8-inch wide crack in the ice. "Good idea," he said.

At 10 p.m. we met in the dining hall for a briefing. In a thick Russian accent, we were instructed to never leave camp alone. Ice can open up at any time, and open water can mean animals such as seals. And when seals are there, "white bear come—for sure."

"Watch friends for white face." That meant frostbite was setting in. Behind the camp were two vinyl outhouses, the holes for which had been dug with a chainsaw. And then there was the pee wall—built of snow blocks, a place where we would find relief for the next three days.

We were now on Moscow time (GMT+4). We were assigned to nine-person tents, approximately 15-by-30 foot structures with a quilted liner and warmth provided by huge salamander heaters located outside between tents. We bedded down for a hot night's sleep.

April 17: Marathon Day. As I looked across the ice toward the helicopters, steam rose. The three-foot lead from the day before had become 100 feet of open water. Nelsen was outside the dining tent waiting to get some video as people assembled for breakfast, and he told me that only a half-hour earlier, he had walked over to the helicopters. It doesn't take long for the ice to move. We went back over to the "river" and discovered a seal playing in the lead. We wondered if we'd get to see a white bear.

At breakfast, we were told we'd be on the second helicopter to the pole at 2:30 p.m. We were learning to distrust time schedules.

We spent the morning playing outside to become acclimatized to our cold environment. A dogsledder named Dag was exercising his dogs by giving us rides. Here I learned dogs don't have to slow down to go potty. Fortunately, gravity near the North Pole works like it does everywhere else, so nothing was going airborne.

Before lunch at 12:30, the first helicopter came over the lead to pick up its North Pole passengers, and suddenly we were informed the marathon group would be going on this flight and had five minutes to get ready. We were beginning to understand why they called them "Rushin'" as we grabbed our bags and headed north, sans one runner, one guide, and one doctor.

We landed about an hour later after dropping two groups along the way for ski expeditions to the pole, and Brent and Richard went out to set up the course—a one-kilometer loop marked with small orange flags that we would run 42 times. After about an hour of preparing, getting dressed, setting up a warming tent, and putting up banners, we were ready.

Around 3 p.m., we got started, running a marathon in the middle of the Arctic Ocean, with only a few inches of ice separating us from the 12,000 feet of frigid ocean below. After a ceremonial loop of 195 meters running together around all the degrees of longitude, we started on the circular course. The dry, crisp snow creaked under our running shoes, providing firm footing for a few steps, alternating with ankle-twisting ridges and soft sugar-like looseness. Every step had the potential of breaking through a crusty layer and burying a leg up to the knee.

At the start, we ran with the wind biting any exposed skin on the right side of our faces. The backstretch was with the wind at our backs, then to the finish with the wind biting the left side. One-quarter of the way was a small mountain (about four feet) quickly carved into a couple steps by runner feet. I dubbed it the Hillary Step, after one of the final obstacles on Mount Everest named after the legendary Sir Edmund Hillary. Brent and Mary switched to snowshoes after a while and became much faster. Along the far side of the course, I saw what looked like a post-hole, where I later found that Dave had broken through the crust and sunk all the way to his knee. I would avoid stepping in it many times in the hours to come.

In the warming tent, snow and ice were being melted *almost* fast enough to keep up with the need for fluids on the course. I hope none of the other runners had any weird diseases, because we all took turns drinking from the same cups and bottles as we made our loops. Warm Gatorade or bouillon soup awaited us at the end of almost every lap.

"Even in cold temps, you lose a lot of moisture, and they couldn't have water bottles just sitting out there for us to use because they would freeze solid," Mary said. "There was this one French scientist there melting ice on a little backpacking stove and was able to keep one bottle available to all the runners. Now, runners aren't modest, and germs and dirt mean nothing, but we all had to share the one bottle. In colder temps, your nose runs more, and all the runny-nose stuff froze on your face, and then you get the bottle for water, so everybody was sticking their frozen snot face into the same bottle and drinking."

After twenty laps, Curtis stopped me to inspect my nose and, seeing that it was turning white, sent me into the tent to get it warmed up. An extremely large Russian helicopter mechanic ripped off my goggles, glasses, and headgear backward over my head, wrapped his giant hand into a ham-like fist, and rubbed my nose with it for about three minutes. He finally stood back and declared, "Is pink." He cleaned the fog off my glasses and goggles, bundled me up, zipped my jacket clear up to my nose, and sent me out to play some more.

The cold was taking its toll as we followed the little flags around and around the course. Halfway around the course for about the twenty-third time, there on the snow in front of me was a rock. Disorientation took a few minutes to clear as I continued around the course. *It's in the middle of a freakin' ocean. There aren't any rocks!* In reality, the call of nature had overtaken one of the runners. Glad I didn't pick it up, though it would have been a humorous gift for my sister.

Martin Tighe, who had trained for this race on a treadmill in a deep-freezer, finished the race in first place, just over five hours. Throughout the race, our Russian hosts had been starting the helicopter periodically to prevent everything from freezing, but with the first finisher in, they were becoming concerned over fuel levels. They suspended the race and hurried us into the helicopter and back to camp, not wanting to risk being stuck at the pole waiting for resupply. Richard managed to finish his last couple laps as runners and gear were loaded into the chopper. The rest of us would have to restart back at camp.

Most of us changed part of our clothing back at camp as Brent set up a 1K out-and-back loop starting at the ceremonial pole and ending at a flag Brent carried out on his first lap. *Only 16K more to go,* I counted down. Dry clothes and rehydrating helped us avoid hypothermia as we resumed our runs. Paul had arrived earlier and joined us, running from 9 p.m. into his thirty-fourth birthday on April 18. Hans VanHeerden, a doctor from Capetown, South Africa, waited a little longer to restart, taking time to warm up some frost-nipped toes.

Halfway out on our new course was a frozen-over crack in the ice, the "Weigner Crack" I called it. It was the only "hazard" on this newly-formed course. Aid was nearly non-existent now, as the race directors were both recovering, and the camp staff had lost interest and gone back to their card playing and vodka drinking. Nelsen did get me some water and even a cup of coffee, but the laps went by faster here and the end was in sight, so aid became less important than just finishing. Counting down, two laps to go.

"God save the Queen!"

Marathon runners say this at the 25-mile mark, which was the length of a marathon at one time. In 1908 at the Olympics, the queen decided to have the starting line moved, making the distance 26.2 miles.

As I finished my penultimate loop, Nelsen told me to do something snazzy for the finish. With 100 yards to go, I unzipped my outer jacket and fleece and took them off. My shirt, by that time wet with sweat, was stuck as I tried to pull my arms out, so I pulled my neck out and got the shirt behind my head to finish bare-chested in the 25-below Arctic air. Brent was there to give me a pat on the stomach after I crossed the line.

April 18: With the main event behind us, it was time for a day of recovery, to enjoy life in the frozen north. The ceremonial North Pole was set up outside the main tent, a striped pole with signs from top to bottom and distances to cities all over the world. As we spent the morning surveying the Arctic ice, it was time for a little more adventure.

Andrey insisted on getting a post-marathon shower, so he stripped to his shorts and dumped a sub-freezing bucket of ocean water over his head, then tipped his head back and dumped half a bottle of Russian vodka down his throat. *I love this guy!* It was my turn to do something crazy, and needing to obtain a picture to match the one I took at the South Pole, I gave my camera to Nelsen, hung my North Pole Marathon shirt over an appropriate-height distance sign, and posed naked behind the ceremonial pole.

Marcus Fillinger, meanwhile, set up a video camera on the ice near one of the leads. He donned a dry suit and SCUBA gear and jumped through the ice to set a record for the world's farthest north solo dive. We spent much of the rest of the day warming up.

Afterward, we packed and then sat in the cooking tent drinking coffee and hot chocolate. Dave's mother sent along some homemade cookies, which had somehow survived the whole trip. They wouldn't survive the morning. Everyone looked forward to heading south, but we had a few more hours to enjoy on the ice.

The flight back to Longyearbyen was scheduled to leave around 12:30 p.m. We went out to spend the rest of the morning on a photo safari as we explored the broken blocks of ice we had dubbed "Ice Henge" and jumped across the various leads around the camp.

Late morning, in an obvious state of aggravation, Richard rounded us up for an impromptu meeting. A group of Australians, who had been scheduled to go out on the flight after us, were using their kids as an excuse for preferential treatment. Instead of returning to Longyearbyen for our post-race celebration, the Aussies would go instead. Under Richard's leadership, we assembled to talk with Curtis, but to no avail.

Soon it was obvious Curtis' karma had run over Richard's dogma, and we would spend another night at Barneo.

While the group was still together, one resourceful runner seized the opportunity and said to Curtis, "Since we have to spend another night here, is it possible we could acquire some alcoholic beverages to celebrate our achievements? At a Russian camp, we should be able to score some vodka or something?" Curtis' face lit up, as he now had an easy way to get back to being a good guy.

"Sure! In fact, I'll even give you my stash." He took me to his tent and gave me a pint bottle of vodka. He also figured he could get us some beer from the Russians.

Richard, Andrey, and Hans left on the 12:30 flight (which actually left around 3:00 p.m.), and the rest of us spent the evening enjoying a small party in the Arctic. Curtis negotiated a 12-pack of Russian beer from our hosts, and Nelsen managed a couple more glasses of vodka as the night wore on. Someone (not me) managed to steal a little more booze from under Curtis' cot.

As we lounged in our tent later that night, Curtis burst into our tent. "Who stole my liquor!" he demanded. He was livid, trying to figure out who had done such a thing, but none of us seemed to know anything about it. After the flight situation earlier in the day, he wasn't able to garner much sympathy. Well, that, and none of us were in much condition to feel sympathetic at the time. The desired effect had set in as the first marathoners at the North Pole enjoyed a pleasant buzz with old and new friends in the frozen arctic.

April 19: Finally, a day with everything on schedule. We headed south to Longyearbyen, got hot showers, and reunited for an evening awards ceremony and meal together. Hans had his nearly frostbitten feet rewarmed by that time and arranged a great post-race banquet. At the end of the evening as Dave, Martin, and I walked back toward the 102, Martin shared some sad news. Returning to Longyearbyen, he got a call that his mother had died on Friday.

The first North Pole Marathon was in the books. On Sunday, we left the airport in Longyearbyen for our long journeys home. We'd lose track of each other as we transferred through airports, stopping for goodbyes on the way through customs and baggage claims, reflecting on our accomplishments and the stories we'd tell our friends back home.

***

Whether it's a strength or a weakness, I'm not sure, but for some reason, I fail to recognize danger when I'm in the middle of it. Still do, actually. While running at the North Pole, there were spots where the ice was thin enough to see bubbles in the water below. The spot where Dave sank his leg in all the way to the knee could have broken a leg very easily in the crusty ice. Life at 25 degrees below zero makes simple problems a lot harder to solve.

In 2004, the Outdoor Life Network contacted me. They were doing one of their Countdown series, the 25 Most Dangerous Places. The final half-hour of the series would count down from number five to the most dangerous place on earth. Number five? The South Pole. Brent and I were featured on that segment. It was my first national TV appearance. In addition to Brent and me, a third person was interviewed, essentially to explain exactly how dangerous the situation actually was. "Some people just find it attractive to take unnecessary risks" is pretty much what he had to say.

Not knowing what I'm getting myself into was also the key to my next (final?) attempt at the world record.

and the adventure continues….

Chapter 14

Maybe We Can Get It Right This Time?

On November 2, 2011, I sat in the boarding area at Washington, D.C.'s Dulles Airport waiting to check in for my flight to South Africa. It had been five and a half years since that fateful day in the coffee shop when I found Tim Rogers' *Guinness World Record* of 99 days to run marathons on all seven continents.

It'd been over four years since I took two cracks at that very record—successfully, but failing to capture the record both times. First, I was beaten by Richard Takata, who had finished all seven in 29 days, 16 hours, and 17 minutes, while I came in just under 35 days. Later in 2007, I compiled a schedule that would have set the record at 25 days, but after completing six marathons, bad weather in the Patriot Hills left me stranded in Punta Arenas, Chile for eight days before I could complete my final run in Antarctica. Again, no record. Sure, I still held the world record for running on all seven continents twice in the shortest amount of time at 307 days, but I couldn't stop dwelling on unfinished business.

So, for the third time, I set off to travel the globe in search of the world record that had proven to be so elusive. I planned to start in Soweto, South Africa, on November 6, and then travel to Ticino, Switzerland; Curitiba, Brazil; Fukuchiyama, Japan; Auckland, New Zealand; Cocoa, Florida; and finally, Antarctica, near the Union Glacier. If all went as scheduled, the new record would be approximately 24 days and 12 hours.

But I knew I had to be ready for the unpredictable.

Africa: Soweto, South Africa—November 6, 2011

I arrived at Tambo International Airport in Johannesburg, South Africa, on November 4 and spent the next two days taking it easy. I looked forward to the days ahead, uncertain of how the adventure would pan out but feeling pretty good about my chances. With a couple days before the marathon, I had the chance to learn of the history of apartheid and the end of that period in South African history. Great strides have been made in South Africa even in my adult lifetime. Enjoying a taxi tour of Johannesburg and Soweto provided a great foundation of familiarity before I embarked on a 26-mile foot tour of the city.

The weather in Soweto was great, and I was ready for a strong opening run. During registration the day before the event, I found my old friends, Jan and Irene van Eeden, whom I had stayed with in Port Elizabeth in 2007. It was nice to see some familiar faces. They were doing the timing for the event. Their presence would prove fortuitous.

The morning of the Soweto Marathon was cool, but not cold. I remained relaxed until I arrived at the race site and discovered I had left my race number in the hotel room. After a few stressful minutes, I found a race official who told me they would have to write it down when I finished. I was pretty sure Jan would be working with the timers at the finish, so I hoped there wouldn't be any problems. Still, it was a stressful few moments. On November 6 at 6 a.m. Soweto time, 4:00 GMT (Greenwich Mean Time, which I keep as the second time zone on my watch and will use to keep track of the journey), the clock started on my third attempt at the record.

As a general rule, I don't know much about a place before going there. Learning on the fly is part of the adventure. The course was quite hilly, but the kilometers still seemed to go by a little slower than I had planned. It wouldn't be until after the race that someone would tell me that the altitude was nearly a mile high. That would account for my heavy breathing along a route that started just outside Nasrec Stadium and headed for downtown Soweto.

Soweto is an interesting study in contrasts. The city has many tin shacks interspersed with brick houses. The average house of the working person is brick and only around 300 to 500 square feet. Many have small tin shacks in the backyard where relatives can live. There were lots of small, roadside stands—some enclosed, some not—that sold varieties of fruits, vegetables, and drinks. "Shade tree mechanic" was a common business here, with signs that advertised services out in the open. Big businesses we're familiar with were everywhere too, like telephone companies and factories. Flags from sponsor Toyota lined the course.

The race continued roughly counter-clockwise around the city, going through the downtown area on Vilakazi Street, the only street in the world with the houses of two Nobel Peace Prize recipients, Bishop Desmond Tutu and Nelson Mandela. Occasionally, runners could be seen far in the distance when our path reached the top of a big climb. Aid stations were stocked with Pepsi, Energade (think Gatorade), and water. The Energade and water came in small plastic bags, to be bitten at one end and squirted into the mouth. It was also convenient to carry an extra one or two along to rehydrate a bit between aid stations. Frequent popping sounds could be heard as people or cars ran over full or partially full bags.

The hills were relentless. After hitting the 38K mark, a left turn revealed the most daunting incline of the day, a stiff climb all the way to the 39K mark. For the first time, I decided to walk for a few minutes, making it the slowest kilometer of the race. As the stadium appeared far in the distance, it wasn't much longer before the final kilometer was upon us.

Approaching the 42K mark with only a couple football fields worth of distance to go, my good friend, Scot McIvor, already finished and on his way to his car, handed me the beer he was less than halfway through and ran with me for about a minute as I enjoyed the rest of the refreshing beverage. It was the third time I had seen Scot during my world record attempts, and a familiar face late in the game is always a boost. My steps felt lighter as I turned into the Nasrec complex toward the finish line. I turned into the stadium for the last couple hundred meters, circling the outside of the field and then down to the finish line, crossing at 5:36:50.

Working my way through the finish chute without a race bib, I scanned the race workers for a familiar Jan, and there he was within yelling distance. I got his attention and told him I forgot my number, and by the time I got to the woman recording the finishes, he was there giving her my bib number. All that stress before the race thankfully turned out to be pretty unnecessary.

Once again, marathon No. 1 was in the books. Now it was off to Switzerland.

Europe: Ticino, Switzerland—November 13, 2011

On Monday, I took an overnight flight to Zurich and then a short flight to Lugano on Tuesday. Lugano is in the Ticino region of Switzerland, very close to Italy. It was a small airport, and the first time I had been on a propeller plane in quite a while. I walked out of the terminal following a sign that said "to trains" and found a shuttle. Good thing I didn't try and walk to the train—it was about a ten-minute ride.

Sometimes when I'm a little unsure of things, I think back to when my friends Paul, Brent, and I landed in South Korea in 2007. Paul had said, "I say we just throw ourselves into the public transportation system and see what happens." Here I was, in another country where I didn't speak the language, throwing myself into the public transportation system yet again. All the signs were in Italian, so I finally gave up and walked inside to buy a train ticket to Locarno, where I would spend the week.

It was a typical fall day, overcast and rainy, so I pulled out my rain jacket and set out to find some tourist info and food. Locarno is located on Lago Magiore, a short distance from the Italian border, and the main shopping district was along the lakeshore and fairly flat. The Hotel Dellavalle in Brione, where I stayed, was way up the hill. I took a taxi there and checked in, and after paying a very large taxi fare, I made sure to ask the hotel owner about my transport options. A bus that ran every half-hour only about 200 meters down the street would provide a far cheaper option. By the way, the bus service there was called Ferrovie Autolinee Regionali Ticinesi and commonly referred to as FART. Apparently, they didn't consult any English-speaking people before coming up with that.

Brione is a friendly place, a small village of about 600 people looking down over Locarno and Lago Magiore. The streets leading down from my hotel were a series of switch-backs to allow cars to travel up and down. Houses and buildings were all built very close together with lots of stonework and tile roofs, both old and new. Few people spoke much English here. No reason to, and nobody understood it anyway. Fortunately, a guy could get a beer pretty handily. I ventured into a couple shops, and the shop owners were friendly, but we had a hard time carrying on any meaningful conversation. I picked up one of the marathon brochures at an information center so at least I had something I could pull out of my pocket and point to so people would know why I was in town.

I was a little nervous for the Maratona Ticino on November 13. I believed I was in shape for a sub-five-hour marathon, and this one actually had a five-hour time limit. Fortunately, the cool fall weather and flat course would provide ideal conditions. With most of the week to prepare, I even managed a couple practice runs, heading straight uphill from my hotel for twenty minutes and then back for twenty minutes. Then I'd walk back up the hill to the hotel to cool down.

There was a small restaurant just down the street from the hotel, where the locals regularly eat and drink. I got a beer at the bar, but for me to eat, the proprietor moved me to a table with a very nice older couple, Margaret and Livio Gaudens, retirees enjoying life in the small community. They spoke enough English to allow us a very pleasant conversation.

On the bus back to the hotel after picking up my race packet on Saturday, I met runners Stefan Luescher and Michael Flueckiger, who were trying to find out how to get to Brione. It turned out they were staying at my hotel, so I guided them all the way there. As they checked into the hotel, I heard some other English-speaking voices, Will Wright and Zara Culican. The five of us got together to enjoy a pre-race meal in the hotel restaurant. Stefan, it turned out, was a pretty fast runner. Will wasn't running, just supporting Zara, but he also offered the rest of us a ride to the race site the next morning. It would be much less stressful than taking the bus.

The field was fairly small, with 186 men and about 40 women. The marathon started at the Central Sports Center in Tenero and headed south and east for the first loop. I had lots of company but didn't really find anyone to run with. I ran pretty well, ahead of my pace in Soweto the previous week. At the 10K point, we went back past the stadium and headed toward Locarno along the lake. Half marathoners started in three waves behind us every fifteen minutes, so occasionally some would come soaring by throughout the first 21K. Soon the course took an uphill turn for about a kilometer, running on the roads a little more than 100 yards from the lake. We reached Locarno, did a loop around town for a couple kilometers, and then hugged the lakeshore back to the stadium. Crossing the finish line and starting out again on the same course for the second half, I checked my watch. About 2:17. Not bad.

The second half started when I crossed the finish line, but suddenly, I was by myself, working my way through pedestrian traffic and hoping I could remember the turns early in the course. There were no course marshals. After leaving the Sports Center, I made a right turn, but something didn't feel right. I turned around and managed to get someone to understand me well enough to point me back to the course. Still, I wasn't sure. It was much easier when there was a whole crowd of runners with me the first time around.

I got part way across a bridge, which I hadn't really noticed when I was among the mass of people at the start, and stopped for a minute. Two women came up behind me who were not in the race but knew where it went, and they pointed me in the right direction. Soon, a sign ahead confirmed I was on course, but the slight detour and resulting confusion cost me about four minutes. I had no time to lose and hopefully had the legs to stay on pace the rest of the time.

Beginning a several-kilometer loop around a big open area, I became aware of a bicycle riding behind me, staying back a few meters but never passing. As irritation set in, I turned around to see a sign on the front of the bike that I managed to translate as "Race Official." The kid on the bike would be my escort for the rest of the day. At least I wouldn't make any more bad turns.

I was all by myself for the second loop. I never caught anyone or saw anyone behind me. I could looked across the field and could see some runners three or four kilometers in front of me, but that was it. After that, it was just me and my own private bicycle escort. He didn't speak a word of English, so there was no conversation to help pass the kilometers. About two-thirds of the way through the second loop, I determined by his brief conversations with course marshals (who must have been anxious to pick up the road cones and go home) that I was the last person in the race. Still, I was easily on pace for sub-five hours.

I did math at every kilometer, knowing if I kept going, I was still on track. The kid was a little inexperienced with escorting, sometimes crowding me or almost cutting me off, but at least he was keeping me on course. Finally, I saw the tops of the Sport Center buildings and the lights of the sports fields. I turned left into the Sports Center, ran past a field house, and made the final turn toward the finish line. I'd finish, first American, but DFL (dead freakin' last) in the race, finishing in 4:56:10. Still, my best time of the year and exactly what I set out to accomplish.

As I went in to watch some of the awards presentations, I saw Michael sitting on a bench watching the ceremony. I asked him what happened to Stefan. He pointed at the stage. Stefan was getting his first place trophy for winning the marathon. The previous night, the first-place runner (Stefan) and the last-place runner (me) had enjoyed dinner together at the Hotel Dellavalle. Interesting things happen sometimes.

It took nearly an hour and a half to work my way back to the hotel via the bus system. I cleaned up, rested for an hour or so, and headed for the train back to Lugano for my flight early the next morning. Monday was a long day of flights, but by evening, I was at home asleep in my own bed.

Thursday, it was back on the road. The next week could be the toughest week of my life. Brazil on Sunday, Japan on Wednesday, New Zealand on Saturday, and Florida on Sunday. I'd either be very satisfied, very disappointed, or dead.

South America: Curitiba, Prana, Brazil—November 20, 2011

I arrived in Curitiba, Brazil, on November 18. Paul's words echoed in my head, and once again, I "threw myself into the public transportation system." I walked out of the airport to see if I could find a shuttle into town. Sure enough, there was one right outside the door. I pointed to the hotel address in my notebook, and the bus attendant circled my stop on the schedule I picked up from the kiosk. After about a half-hour through lots of traffic, some new friends from the bus saw the confusion on my face and made sure I got off at the right stop. They even pointed out my street when I got off the bus and made sure I headed in the right direction.

Only about three blocks later, I arrived at my hotel. After a walk around town to get oriented, I headed to a little bar not far from the hotel for something to eat. Most places seemed to have someone in the back room who knew a passable amount of English, and with their help, I was able to pull enough information off the Portuguese menu to fill up and have a bottle of Xingu, one of the Brazilian beers.

The desk clerk at the hotel gave me a tourist map and a little instruction about where we were, then told me the location of the packet pickup was about a thirty-minute ride via taxi. I walked instead. After about fifty minutes, I found the mall where it was located. Once again, I found myself in a country where almost nobody speaks English. They were all pretty friendly, however, and if we couldn't understand one other, there was someone nearby that they could summon for help. That was the case at the running store, as I stood in line for my race packet. I had sent in the information, but needed to pay for my entry when I got there. The mall was like every mall in the U.S. Same stores, different names, but the same stuff. Coffee shops, McDonald's, Burger King. Next door was a Sam's Club.

I thought about how the whole world is essentially the same. Maybe that's an over-simplification, but after being in a lot of different countries, it becomes apparent how similar we really are. Everyone wants the same stuff from stores: food, clothing, entertainment, bread and milk, soap, etc. McDonald's, KFCs, and Subways—fast food is virtually the same everywhere.

In Brazil, there were Catholic churches, Jewish temples, and Islamic mosques everywhere. People held hands, played with their kids, and looked for work. Some were rich, some were poor, some were homeless. The women dressed to look nice, and the men looked at them. I'm thinking I could live most anywhere and figure out how to make it. I may have to learn a new language or something, but even the languages are expressing the same thoughts all over the world.

Okay, Antarctica isn't going to have a McDonald's. Or a brewery (Darn it!). But most everywhere else will.

The Curitiba Marathon was held on November 20. I had to arrive early that morning to pick up my timing chip, which would be distributed at the race site. It was nice to arrive early and relax. I even found a few people who could speak a little English to talk to before the race. One guy I met had run the Space Coast Marathon in Florida a couple years earlier. If all went according to plan, I'd run this marathon and two more and be at Space Coast in seven days. The thought was nearly overwhelming.

The race had a six-hour time limit, so that made me relax a little more. Good thing, too, because with about 2,900 feet of elevation and lots of hills, I'd need the extra time. To pace myself for this adventure, I needed to think about recovery from the start to the finish to make this whole thing work. Kilometers go by a lot faster than miles, so even on a slow day, benchmarks came more quickly.

As I got to the first aid station, volunteers handed me a plastic cup full of water, sealed on top with foil. I tried to peel the foil off. That didn't work. Finally, I jammed my finger through it, splashing water all over the place. It got better as I learned the technique of just puncturing it enough to drink. It was also good because I could carry an extra cup along and drink whenever I wanted. Gatorade in small portions was served at about every second aid station.

Curitiba is known as a garden city, and like many other things in Brazil, the gardens are nicely trimmed. Buildings and houses are built touching each other, so it can be hard to find a place to discreetly make a pit stop. I fell into a steady but not too speedy pace and felt pretty good. As I got through the first half in about 2:43, I knew I was slowing down a bit, but so were the people ahead of me. At the 18K mark, I spotted a girl in an orange shirt with a bicycle escort. She managed to stay just ahead of me for most of the rest of the race, but between the 40 and 41K markers, I finally caught her and her escort, who had somehow ditched the bicycle and was running alongside her.

"I've been chasing you for a long time," I said as I passed her.

Both she and her friend laughed, maybe because they understood me (few people do in this country) or maybe just because I look funny or something. We turned the corner and made the final push for the finish line.

As we approached the finish, more and more people with orange shirts came out and yelled for their friend behind me. It was her first marathon, and her running club was there to share the celebration. I picked it up to finish in front of her rather than be run over by her entourage, and I finished in about 5:48. I turned around to congratulate my new friend on her first marathon, then went to get my medal and grab some food. I had a few hours to rest, pack, and get to the airport. In about sixty hours, I would be running in Japan.

Every adventure comes with a little fear—not knowing what will happen, if you're up to the task, if everything will happen on time. I'd had my share of those feelings during this adventure. After running a strong marathon in Switzerland, I had so much knee pain that I didn't run a step during the week between marathons, a rarity for me. It wasn't until the day before my race in Brazil that my knee felt good enough for me to know I would be fine, but I wore a neoprene sleeve over it for extra support.

My biggest fright came the day before the Curitiba Marathon, after I sent a message to my contact in Japan asking for some information. The entry form I sent in the first part of August never hit the organizer's email, so he didn't even know I was coming. I was supposed to report to the trouble desk to pay when I got there, and I figured I was all set. He told me to send it again immediately, but right after that, he mentioned that the entry period had ended. I sent it to him again through two different email services just to be safe, but since it was already the weekend there, he didn't respond. I tried calling, but of course, the office was closed.

With my mission in question, it weighed on my mind all weekend, occupying my thoughts as I ran the marathon in Curitiba, keeping me awake on the plane. Finally, during a layover at the airport in Frankfort, Germany, I received an email letting me know everything was approved. The last time I felt so relieved was October 31, 2004, the moment when the starting gun went off and the inaugural Grand Rapids Marathon was underway.

I was sure there would be a couple more moments like that before the end of the adventure, but for the time being, everything was on schedule.

Asia: Fukuchiyama, Japan—November 23, 2011

Forty-two hours after I left my hotel in Curitiba, I arrived in Fukuchiyama, Japan, on Tuesday, November 22. My contact, Nobohito Isono from the race staff, didn't just recommend a hotel, he made a reservation.

After flying Curitiba to Sao Paulo to Frankfort to Osaka, it was a three-hour train ride to Fukuchiyama. I arrived at the train station and was trying to figure out how to get to my hotel. Everything I could find was in Japanese characters, so figuring out where to go was proving, well, next to impossible. There was a big guide map in the train station, and fortunately the hotels had phone numbers on the map. Arabic numerals! I could read them!

As I stood at the board locating my hotel by way of phone number with my confused-tourist-where-the-&%$#-am-I look, a man came over to help. His English wasn't great, but we could communicate. I pointed to my hotel on the sign, and he tried to direct me, then gave up and motioned to follow him. We walked the block or so to the hotel, and I was able to tell him what I was doing.

When we got there, it turned out the hotel was overbooked and they had moved me to a hotel on the other side of the station. He took the paper from the clerk, told me we needed to go to another hotel, and walked back through the train station and out the other side with me to the R Hotel. He had a long conversation with the clerk there, made sure I was checked in, and then said goodbye. Domo arigato!

I hadn't slept a lot during the previous forty-plus hours. My last five meals and two nights of lodging were provided by airlines. I looked forward to an actual bed. A hot shower also felt great. My body wasn't sure what time it was, but I actually felt well fed and fairly recovered from the previous marathon.

In my experience, the best way to recover from jet lag is to get up and run a marathon in the morning. It's easy to get yourself feeling on schedule. The GI tract takes a couple days to catch up, though. It bothers me more mentally than physically, I think, because race morning elimination just isn't the same. (That's all I have to say about that sh*t.)

I felt a little anxious the next morning for marathon number four. The time limit was six hours, and after running only two days before in Curitiba, I wondered how my legs would feel. The race shuttle was in sight when I walked out the front door of the hotel, right outside the train station, so getting to the race was easy.

My first task was to find the "Trouble Desk" and pay for my race entry. After passing the numbered packet pickup tables, I found something that looked like it could be the right place. The problem was that very few in this area spoke English, so it took us a while to agree it was the trouble desk and then to figure out what I was trying to do there. Finally, they found my number, called Isono, and told me to wait. I was finally able to meet the man who had helped me so much the past few days. He took me over to the bag pickup, showed me where the gym and facilities were, then headed back to work.

It was nearly three hours before the race start. It wasn't very busy yet, so I walked around, found a row of chairs in a hallway near the gym, and snoozed a bit. I had a protein bar for breakfast, but I was a little concerned that I hadn't eaten more or had enough to drink, since the start was so late in the day.

We started at 10:30 a.m., and by the time I crossed the start line, the clock was already at the five-minute mark. We started with a loop around the downtown area and crossed the 5K mat. The first aid station followed, and I took a minute to drink quite a bit to catch up on my hydration. As we worked our way out of town, we turned left close to the 12K point for a long out-and-back. The 40K marker was just after the corner, so as I went along, I figured the turn would be between 24K and 25K.

As we continued out of town, it felt as if we were running downhill most of the time. Believing that, I tried to stay steady, anticipating a long 17K worth of climbing after the turnaround. There were a couple uphill sections, but it felt predominantly like we were working our way down the valley. The course followed a river valley nestled in the mountains, with great views in the distance. In spite of the mountains, the elevation wasn't very high above sea level.

I reached the halfway point in under 2:30. Right on schedule. I made the turn at three hours on the clock, and right after passing the 25K mats, there was a party. Men were beating huge drums, and there was a row of tables with hot chocolate, hot tea, and little triangles of sticky rice. My split on that kilometer suffered a bit as I enjoyed the culinary treats.

Remember when our parents were young, and they had to walk 10 miles to school, uphill both ways? This is where we made up for it because even after the turn, it still seemed as if we were going downhill. In fact, there were a few hills on the way back, but they had looked a lot worse on the way out. The hill at 30K was not as severe as I anticipated.

Somewhere in the next couple of kilometers was another party. The locals were out with tables full of goodies, and I spotted two bottles of wine with empty cups hanging on top of them. What the heck, I was ahead of schedule. I stopped for a glass of wine, which my hosts took great joy in watching me drink. Judging from their surprised reaction, I may have been the first to enjoy their liquid hospitality. More people were passing out candy and little treats along the way, but I skipped most of them and tried to concentrate on keeping a steady pace.

Back at the 40K mark, we made the left turn that indeed took us uphill for the final two kilometers. The climbing didn't matter. I felt great. It surprised me how many people were walking by that time. I turned the final corner and crossed the finish line, finishing in a net time of just over 5:21.

It was after 7 p.m. by the time I arrived back at the hotel, and I went down the street and looked at enough pictures on a menu to order a delicious post-race meal. The next morning, the train took me back to Osaka, where I would embark for New Zealand.

The flight from Japan to New Zealand was delayed by about thirty minutes, and with a short connection in Gold Coast, Australia, I was a little concerned about both me and my suitcase making it to the correct destination. Fortunately, there were no problems. After three hours on a train from Fukuchiyama to Osaka, eight hours overnight to Gold Coast and three more hours to Auckland, I landed in New Zealand on November 25.

Oceania: Bethel's Beach, west of Auckland, New Zealand— November 26, 2011

New Zealand is probably my favorite country to visit. Kiwis have a great attitude, and it's pretty much the adrenaline capital of the world. If you want to bungee jump, sky dive, whitewater raft, or just hike the tracks and camp, it's a great place to be. I had one of the best Christmases ever in Queenstown back in 1999 on the Millennium Marathon trip. I wished I had a few more days to spend there, but duty called.

I didn't get much sleep on the way from Japan, but I felt pretty good.

I drove out to check the race site first thing, then back closer to town to find a place to stay and a good pre-race steak dinner. The marathon started at 7:30 a.m. the next day. It would be my third marathon of the week on my third different continent, and fifth overall. My mission was to get through the 42.2K worth of trails, probably in around seven or eight hours, then get cleaned up and back to the airport. My total time in New Zealand was scheduled to be about thirty-one hours.

Instead, the series of events that followed nearly derailed my whole record attempt.

The Speight's West Coaster Marathon is the toughest trail run I've ever done. Keep in mind I've run Pikes Peak in Colorado a couple times, the Inca Trail to Machu Picchu in Peru, and the Six Foot Track in Australia. Those were child's play compared to this event.

I met Rachel and Mark from near Sydney, Australia, in line while picking up my race number, and we talked about my mission. I didn't know at the time how instrumental Rachel would be in my race.

The race started straight into extreme winds toward the beach. Wow. Before we ever got started, I wondered what I had gotten myself into. After running south for a while, we turned off the beach and started climbing. I was in last place and trying to keep someone in sight at least. Even that was tough. As we started into the hills, I was able to catch up a little bit with the last couple. It was Rachel and Mark. After a couple kilometers, Rachel told Mark to go ahead.

"The crazy man's right behind me; I'll just go with him," she said.

We worked our way around the first 12K loop, which was a good run, but it seemed longer than 12K and ended with the last kilometer going right down the middle of a stream. It took us about 2:15 total for that segment and got us to the first aid station.

It turned out to be the easiest of the four segments.

The second section, 10K on the Hillary Trail, featured a lot of climbing. After climbing for about a half-hour or better, working our way around a mountain, we looked up to our left.

"I hope we don't have to go all the way to the top of that," I said to Rachel, and she quickly agreed.

Then we looked a little closer and saw little tiny people on the trail at the top of the mountain. *(Expletive deleted), I guess we're climbing.* We kept going for what seemed forever, and about two thirds of the way through the 10K segment, runners started coming back at us. The half and the 30K were out and back on this piece of the course, so they were on their way back. On the narrow trails, we had to squeeze past people regularly, which slowed us down even more. Finally, we reached the second aid station. It would be a long day.

Segment three was another 10K segment, which started out down a road, then on to a nicely groomed trail, then down about 30 sets of steps. We met runners coming back up the steps, so we knew it would be tough coming back. What we didn't know was what was still coming. Rachel had gone ahead by that time, running faster on the smooth trails.

At the bottom of the steps, we reached a bridge, but instead of crossing, the course turned right, then circled under the bridge and started upstream. I soon caught Rachel after a couple stream crossings, and once again, we worked together trying to keep our eyes on the marked trail, back and forth across the stream. For the next hour, we fought our way along the course, losing the marker ribbons as we paid more attention to footing than we did to the trail. We followed the ribbons back and forth, frequently backtracking to find the trail we kept losing.

Before we reached the end of the stream bed, the bill of my cap blocked my view of a branch as I looked down, and SMACK! My glasses bent as my head bashed into the branch and created a nice little bruise below my right eye. I pressed the hinge of my glasses against a tree trunk and almost got it bent into a position where my eyes would work together again, then finally finished the stream section. But now we had to go back up the steps.

My 7:30 p.m. flight loomed large in my mind, as I started to doubt I could make it in time. However, missing the flight would be irrelevant if I didn't finish the race, so we pressed on.

We eventually left the stream and headed back up a series of steps. They weren't the steps we remembered, though. Soon we came to an intermediate drink station that wasn't in the course description. We thought we were going to make it back to aid station No. 2 by the 2 p.m. cutoff, but it turned out it was still a long way off. We went down more steps to the bridge, crossed, and started back up the steps we had come down earlier.

By the time we reached the station, it was 2:37 p.m., and Paul, one of the staff, said, "I hate to tell you this, but you're going to have to get a ride back." I explained I had no choice but to finish, and had to go. Rachel sold them on the idea that she was my pacer, and we went off toward the finish with Paul's blessing. Soon he would follow behind us to take down the marking ribbons.

We felt like we were making better time as we headed back over the 10K section of the Hillary Trail, but it was still tough going. There were lots of severe downhill sections, along with a lot more climbing. A little over halfway back, it became mostly downhill. Paul had joined us after about three kilometers and was great at letting us know where we were and how much farther it was. He called ahead to the finish to tell them of my mission and to make sure they saved a beer or two.

About 3K before the end, I was still moving fairly well, but Rachel stopped for a drink and was slow getting started again. Paul stayed back with her, and I went on ahead. A final push, and I was back on flat ground for the last kilometer back to base. I waded through one final tidal pool, got back to Bethel's Beach, and finished continent number five somewhere just over nine and a half hours, my slowest marathon finish ever.

After taking more than nine hours to finish the marathon—only my running companion, Rachel, and one other person finished behind me—I ate a quick snack, washed it down with a beer, took a quick rinse in the outdoor "wash off the beach sand" shower at the race site, and bolted for the airport for my 7:30 p.m. flight. It would be tight, but I thought I had a chance.

I parked the rental car, shoved my dripping wet shoes into the water bottle pockets of my backpack, left my drenched, dirty socks for someone to throw away, and shoved anything else I wanted to keep into my bag. Inside, I breezed by the rental counter, handing the attendant my keys, and without stopping forward progress, told him I probably missed my flight already, that they needed to put gas in it and add it to my bill.

I got to the check in line at 7:10 p.m., but the "traffic director" there said there was no way I could make it. I knew that already, but my heart sank just the same. Marathon six of seven was the next day, and my hopes of getting there were closing with the boarding doors. She sent me across the aisle to the Air New Zealand counter to figure out something.

My flight was booked through Continental, and they put me to Los Angeles on the later ANZ flight but couldn't get me to Orlando until 3:30 Sunday afternoon. Unfortunately, the Space Coast Marathon in Cocoa, Florida, was at 6:15 Sunday morning, and for the plan to work, I had to be there. It wasn't possible for the agent to get me there on time.

I wasn't done yet.

"Okay, get me to my own country, and I'll figure something out." But in my head, I was saying, "Really? I'm Marathon Don. Now stand the f*ck back and watch this!" Okay, I'm a guy. So, naturally, sometimes I want to think I'm a superhero.

With five of the seven continents complete, the fatigue, the thousands of miles traveled and the thousands of dollars spent, along with the very real possibility of failure, I should have been a wreck. Instead, I was surprisingly calm. In the face it all, there was one thing that never occurred to me:

Giving up.

As I checked in for the flight, the agent printed my boarding pass. When she asked about my bag, I looked at her and said, "Check it to LAX."

Chapter 15

And The New World Record Is . . .

---///---

Captain Jean Luc Picard of the starship *Enterprise* once said, "Things are only impossible until they're not!" He may be a fictional character living more than 300 years from now, but in my "List of Rules," his quote still earns a prominent place. "We can't get you into Orlando before Sunday at 3:30 p.m." represented an impossibility that was totally unacceptable.

I went through security and customs at the Auckland airport, then found a place to sit with my computer. Searching the available connections, I found one that would let me hook up and buy an hour worth of Internet access. I searched every travel site I knew of, finally finding one option. US Airways had a flight into Orlando that arrived at 4:51 a.m. Sunday. The Space Coast Marathon was set to start at 6:15 a.m. According to Google Maps, it was a forty-minute drive to the race from

Orlando to Cocoa. It would be a tight schedule, but it might just work. I took out my credit card.

With a new ticket and some renewed hope, I called Francine in Florida. "How can you be on the phone right now?" she wondered aloud when she heard my voice, knowing I was supposed to be on a plane. We wouldn't be spending Saturday night together as planned, but she would make my marathon the next morning a reality.

For some reason, in spite of spending nearly ten hours beating through the trails of New Zealand and an exhaustingly stressful trip to the airport, sleep eluded me on the eleven-hour flight from Auckland to Los Angeles. The on-demand TV in the seat-back screen allowed me to watch a couple movies and six episodes of *Chicago Code* as we flew across the International Date Line, experiencing my second Friday night and Saturday of the weekend, heading north and east across the Pacific. Somewhere over the Pacific, an hour or so of sleep caught up with me, but apparently I was too keyed up to give in to The Sandman for very long.

At LAX, I retrieved my bag, abandoned my Continental Airlines boarding pass for the flight that would have taken me to Orlando by Sunday afternoon, and checked in at the US Air counter. The upgrade to first class for the trip from L.A. to Orlando wasn't too expensive, so I paid for it, hoping for a better sleeping environment. I caught a few minutes of sleep at the gate and maybe a half-hour or so on the way to Phoenix. At the Phoenix airport, I commandeered a handicapped stall and put my running clothes on under my street clothes. The dry airplane air had my running shoes closer to wearable, but they were still pretty damp. I'd put them on in Cocoa later. I grabbed a 12-inch roast beef sub with extra meat from Subway for some much needed protein and nourishment before the next morning.

I was dead asleep before we took off from Phoenix, and oblivious to the fact that they left us on the runway for more than a half-hour while dealing with some kind of maintenance delay. Other than an occasional interruption from a screaming kid nearby, I was finally calm enough to sleep for much of the flight, maybe another two and a half hours.

At 4:50 a.m., I could see the Gulf coastline of Florida out the window, and I thought, *Wait a minute, we're supposed to be landing now!* I sat, helpless to do anything but wonder how much later we would be. It was 5:20 a.m. by the time we touched down, and nearly 5:30 when I finally walked off the plane. (For perspective, it was already 11:30 p.m. Sunday night in New Zealand.) The forty-minute drive to Cocoa meant being late for the start was no longer a question. It was reality.

Needing to get out of the airport as quickly as possible, the first stop was the rental car counter. The rental car company I had reserved with was at the far end, so I didn't bother walking that far, picking the nearest one instead.

"I need a car with a GPS and one of those boxes that lets you blow through toll booths without stopping," I said, trying to keep the urgency in my voice from becoming too apparent.

Then it was back to baggage claim where the crowd was gone and my bag was all by itself going around the carousel. In my car, I set the GPS for the address of the race. It said one hour and twenty minutes to get there—someone had it set to avoid toll roads. Fortunately, I knew the straight-line route was a lot shorter, and by the time I reached the race site, the little electronic lady in the GPS was pretty pissed about being ignored.

North America: Space Coast Marathon, Cocoa, Florida, USA—November 27, 2011

As luck would have it, Route 528 is about the only straight road in all of Florida, and it's also the road to Cocoa. It was dark, and fortunately there was no traffic—and even more fortunately, no cops. I drove eighty miles-per-hour toward marathon number six. I remembered I had my running clothes on under my street clothes, so I set the cruise control and undressed while speeding down the freeway. (Don't try this at home, kids.)

Meanwhile, at the race site was my not-so-secret weapon: The Lovely Francine. As the race was getting ready to start, she was schmoozing the race director and the timer. After the race started, she occupied the official timers and explained what I was doing, where I was, and what was at stake. The timing mats were being picked up to be moved to the finish line, but Francine successfully convinced them to leave one in place. The marathon had a seven-hour cutoff, so even with a late start, if I could just get there within an hour, there was still hope.

The moment I first called Francine the night before, she knew something was wrong. If only it had been that simple.

"My heart sank because I thought he wasn't going to make it," Francine said. "But when he said 'I'm on a plane to get me to Los Angeles, and I'm going to see what I can do to get there,' for me it was, 'All right, what can I do to make this work?'"

She had managed to talk to the race director the day before at the marathon expo to provide a heads-up and let them know about my record attempt, but when I told her I wouldn't even land until nearly 5 a.m., she went into action – again.

"My mind was always, 'What can I do to make this happen?' I didn't think about anything else," she said. "I actually thought about a clean hat for him—I don't know why. I got his race bib and put all the pins in the corners so when he got there, he just had to attach it and go.

"As soon as the last person crossed the starting line, I found the timers and said, 'Okay, this is the situation. Can you leave this mat going? Can you leave the clock going so he has a start time?' At first, their comment was, 'We really can't, but if you keep track of what time you cross, call me and I'll make sure it's written down.' I was worried this might not be good enough, and I didn't want this to mess it up, so I was really quite adamant about it. I stood there and waited. Finally, this guy looks at me and says 'When is he going to be here?' At that point, I said he just called, he's driving, he'll be here in ten minutes, and the guy left it going. That was a big relief."

At 6:15 a.m., about the time I was exiting Route 528 onto I-95, the starting gun sounded and 900 marathoners ran around the block, then headed north along Indian River Drive. As I wheeled into town just after 6:30, the crowd was cleared out, with only cops on the corner still watching traffic. I found a place to park, slipped my almost-dry shoes on, and headed toward the nearest cop, yelling "Which way to the starting line?" After telling me the race had already started (duh!), I asked him again and he pointed me down the street.

People were still milling about as I tried to pick Francine out of the crowd. I was practically on top of her before seeing her, as she and the official race timer were conversing as they waited. He had left one of the timing mats, and assured me there was no hurry. Francine handed me my race bib and my timing chip, and I attached the chip to my shoe. About twenty-five minutes after the rest of the pack had started, Francine and I officially started the Space Coast Marathon. I got a lump in my throat, finally allowing myself to get just a little bit emotional after solving all the problems of the last thirty hours or so.

Tradition dictates we share a hug and kiss before we start marathons. Neither of us even thought of that. Instead, we took off, not knowing where the course went, yelling semi-panicky questions at every corner, trying to get on course until after a half-mile, we rounded the first block and turned onto Indian River Drive. Soon we saw a mile marker. Then an aid station. Then, somewhere in the next mile or so, it occurred to us, "Didn't we forget something?" We stopped where we were and took care of business before continuing our journey.

Marathon No. 6 was happening.

After spending the previous day climbing, wading, and bushwhacking through New Zealand, the flat, paved course was easy. We figured there would be some walkers near the back of the pack, and sure enough, after about 4.5 miles, we finally saw someone ahead of us. At about the same time, the leaders started coming back at us as well. Francine stayed with me the whole way, even though it was probably painfully slow for her. Still, she stuck right by my side. It took us all the way to the turnaround, nearly 7 miles, to figure out how the course worked. We caught up to a guy who told us the course went back to where we started and then on a long out and back to the south.

In spite of being on my feet for nine and a half hours the day before and trying to sleep on airplanes for two nights—crossing the dateline had given me an extra-long Saturday—the day was going well. Starting at the back of the pack was great, and for the first time ever, no one passed me during a marathon. Francine and I paced together, picking off one runner after another all the way through the race. Partying spectators around mile 19 gave me a beer out of their cooler, which made that bit of the course ever so much more enjoyable.

After fighting so hard for every kilometer in New Zealand, the flat, paved roads of Florida felt like a party. We passed people right up to the end. In a little over five and a half hours, we finished marathon number six, "impossible" only thirty hours earlier. Captain Picard would have been proud!

As we enjoyed post-race refreshments that included sausage, eggs, and pancakes, the announcer, who had apparently been talking to Francine earlier as well, told my story to the crowd. I made my way up to the stage, and then right behind me came the legendary Katherine Switzer, the first woman ever to officially enter the Boston Marathon, to congratulate me and give me a hug. Wow, one of my running heroes!

Twenty-six-point-two is tough, no matter how you do it, but the events of the previous couple days made the Space Coast Marathon feel pretty easy in comparison. Staying around in Florida for a bit and enjoying the Kennedy Space Center and the company of my favorite woman in the whole world (not necessarily in that order) would have been great. But the adventure had to continue.

After cleaning up and hurrying to the airport for my next flight, for the second time in as many days I turned in a rental car without filling the gas tank. The woman at the AeroMexico counter looked up as I arrived to check in and said, "Hello, Mr. Kern." That was something I hadn't heard during the past few marathons. Being a race director and fairly well known in marathon circles, I'm frequently asked, "Hey, aren't you Don Kern?" This time, though, it wasn't because of my reputation. It was because I was the only person not yet checked in for the flight. I was famous by process of elimination, I guess. There was still a little time to spare, but not very much.

The flight from Orlando went first to Mexico City, then on to Santiago, Chile, where LanChile Airlines would return me once more to Punta Arenas, my South American home away from home. The mission was almost complete.

Antarctica; Antarctic Ice Marathon, Union Glacier Camp, Ellsworth Mountains

Excitement was building. Past experience, however, told me Antarctica is the proverbial fat lady that doesn't always sing on schedule.

It was nice to be in Punta Arenas that Monday, if only to sleep horizontally on a bed for the first time in about three days. Checking in to the Diego de Almagro Hotel was comfortingly familiar, and after a quick shower to rinse off the travel, I ventured down to the hotel restaurant and found one of my best friends and travel companions, Brent Weigner, enjoying a bottle of Chilean wine. Before the evening was over, others would help us enjoy several more bottles of said wine.

The next morning, somewhere around 7 a.m., was the originally planned time to head out for the White Continent. Already we had been alerted to the likelihood of a short delay. Tuesday morning, November 29, there was a scheduled update between 6:30 and 9:30 a.m. At 9:15 a.m., Antarctic Ice Marathon race director Richard Donovan, my other "bi-polar" friend, informed us it would be delayed until 1:30 p.m. Still, we were optimistic about being able to travel that day.

By the way, Brent and Richard are the two guys I refer to as my bi-polar friends. I've been to both poles with them, the South Pole in 2002 and the North Pole in 2003. That they would both be with me for the end of this adventure was a real treasure.

In previous visits to the interior of the frozen continent, the most important lesson learned was that patience is the best asset. Things rarely happen on schedule in the most inhospitable place on earth. An afternoon departure could easily mean the day after tomorrow. I walked into the center of Punta Arenas to pick up some sunscreen and returned in time for the next briefing, which actually came in around noon. Again, no go.

The next attempt would be 4:30 p.m., so I headed out to grab some lunch with a group of guys who hailed from Wisconsin, Poland, the Czech Republic, the Netherlands, and Germany. A couple beers and a burger at Lomit's (a burger and beer joint Brent and I first visited together in 2002) were just what we needed.

We were originally scheduled to fly to Antarctica in the early morning on November 29 and run on November 30, but every update slowed the mission just a little more. We were officially in wait-and-see mode. The scenario was way too familiar. Winds that blow across a blue-ice runway in Antarctica to keep it clear can rapidly shift and fill it in with snow, making it unusable for days. The next thing that happens is you're seeing all the tourist sites in southern Chile, killing time while waiting to go to Antarctica. Deep in the pit of my stomach was an uneasy feeling. *I don't know if I can do all this a fourth time.*

At 6:55 p.m., the welcomed news spread among the runners: Meet in the lobby at 7:30 p.m. to get on the bus. We packed up, checked out, and loaded the bus for the airport. In the history of the Antarctic Ice Marathon, this was the first time in the history of the event that the plane would fly out on the day it was scheduled. It was the eight-day delay due to an unusual period of snow in 2007 that derailed my previous world record attempt.

I breathed a huge sigh of relief, knowing at least we would be in position to run the marathon with minimal delays. Running on November 30 looked doubtful, but we were easily on time for the next day. At least we would be in the right place. Once again, I positioned myself with the cargo in a Russian Ilyushin 76 plane. The whine of the engines grew to a deafening roar, and finally the crew pulled in the ladder and closed the door. We lifted off and headed south, looking to touch down at Union Glacier about four and a half hours later.

At 2:20 a.m., wheels glided onto the blue ice runway. After coasting for what seemed forever, the Ilyushin slowed to a stop, and the door opened to the vast whiteness. Most in the group took their first look at Antarctica, stepping down the ladder from the plane at the Union Glacier "airport."

For me, it was a like returning to old stomping grounds.

We were escorted to a small building that served as the waiting area for the vehicles that would shuttle us approximately eight kilometers to camp. We chatted with some of the climbers who had just come back from climbing Mount Vinson, Antarctica's highest peak. Raw noses, severely chapped lips, and sunburnt faces were the norm among the climbers who waited there to board the plane for the return to Punta Arenas.

We loaded into huge four-wheel drive vehicles (think Jeeps on steroids) and were transported to camp. Halfway there, we saw little orange flags, and an occasional mile marker as the "road" we were on ran alongside the marathon course we would shortly be running.

The first order of business at the camp was a short briefing about the restrooms. Because everything is kept as pristine as possible, all our waste would be transported back to South America for disposal, so liquids and solids were kept separate. All the other waste at the camp was similarly disposed of, leaving nothing behind to pollute the environment. After we were all potty trained, we went into the dining tent for hot drinks and cookies.

We waited for our luggage and sleeping bags to be brought from the plane until nearly 5:30 a.m., so two hours before breakfast, we finally got some sleep. The marathon wouldn't happen as scheduled on November 30, given the late hour of our arrival, but at least we were in place.

Our accommodations were double-walled clamshell tents equipped with beds, a table, towel, washcloth, soap, and washbasin. Because it's daylight twenty-four hours a day, the sun kept the inside of the tent fairly warm (probably in the 40s F.), even uncomfortably so on a clear day. At 10:30 a.m., it was time to get up and walk around a bit. Given the late hour of our arrival, the marathon wouldn't take place until the next day, December 1. It was a few weeks early, but right then I felt like a kid on the night before Christmas. If everything stayed on schedule, almost four days would come off the world record. Sleeping would be hard that night.

Anticipation built as we enjoyed our morning breakfast, then camp staff briefed us of our itinerary. They wanted to start the race at 11 a.m. I left the post-breakfast briefing to prepare myself for the run.

At 10:30 a.m., we piled onto a huge sled behind the snow-cat tractor for the drive to the starting line, approximately 5 miles from base camp. The course was on a 25K loop—roughly a triangle, with a 6-mile leg on the far side to the first checkpoint, 5 miles back to camp for checkpoint two, and back out to the starting line for checkpoint three. We'd repeat the first two segments to bring us back to camp and the finish line. It was about 7 degrees with a clear sky and plenty of sunshine.

We made sure to gather all our gear and make all the last-minute adjustments, including applying plenty of sun block. Bins with personal items and food were transported to the two checkpoints that were located at the far corners of the course, but I didn't send anything. I just put some extra gloves, a hat, a neck gaiter, and a couple snacks in my waist pack. I planned to start with my windbreaker and take it off as soon as I started to sweat. Sweat is a killer in cold climates, and after seven or eight hours, being wet and cold could rapidly turn life-threatening.

At 11:17 a.m., December 1, 2011, Richard Donovan blew the starting whistle, and the Antarctic Ice Marathon was underway. Only 26.2 miles separated me from the record book as we started out on the long backstretch of the 25K loop course. Everything ahead of us was flat and white, and the faster runners (i.e., almost everybody else) were disappearing into the distance ahead of me. The mile markers were small, close to the ground, and not visible until only a couple hundred yards away. The snow was firm underfoot, but unlike pavement, every push-off would loosen the hard packed surface under our toes, making shorter-than-normal strides.

Soon the 16-mile mark appeared in the distance, but that mile marker was for the second time around. The 1-mile marker appeared shortly afterward, about fifteen minutes after the starting whistle. The combination of activity, sunshine and nearly still air warmed me up in a hurry. I took off my wind jacket to slow down the sweat. 25 miles to go.

It didn't take long for the row of runners to turn into mere colored dots against the vast sea of whiteness in the distance, as I worked my way down the long, straight trail. I'd be running by myself most of the day. Even with the ideal conditions, the groomed snow trails still provided difficult footing in spots. I didn't know how long that back section of the course was, but I did know it was a straight shot to the first checkpoint. The fifteen-minute first mile was my fastest of the day.

The scenery changed little, only white punctuated with little red flags every 200-300 feet. The lack of landmarks made each mile seem endless, and the far-off mountains never came any closer. After passing the 5-mile marker, the first aid station—still a mile away—appeared in the distance. In the clear, crisp air, it appeared close, but it was a long trek to get there.

I arrived just as Sebastian, a runner from Argentina, was getting ready to leave, and found the checkpoint well stocked with warm water to mix with powdered sport drink, as well as cookies, chocolate, dried fruit and various snacks set out in bowls. Because I didn't want to carry a water bottle with me—it would just freeze anyway—I stayed at the aid station long enough to drink several glasses of liquids and eat a few snacks. A wall of snow blocks had been built as our own private "port-a-john," and I made my way around it to pee into a funnel stuck in the top of a small plastic barrel. No peeing in the snow is allowed; we keep Antarctica pristine.

The course turned to the right to leave the station, and I made off after Sebastian in the general direction of Union Glacier camp, which I estimated to be about 5 miles away. My mile times leveled out at a little more than seventeen minutes, and just before getting back to our base camp, I caught up with two of the women. A couple hundred feet before crossing under the finish line banner for the first time, I passed the 11-mile marker. Four of us were together at the second checkpoint, which was equally as well stocked as the first but with lots more people from the camp coming out to cheer us on. I kept the stop down to about five minutes and left ahead of Sebastian as he took advantage of the nicest facilities on the course rather than waiting to use the "snow toilet" at the next checkpoint.

The third segment went a little more than 4 miles, back to where we started the race. Off in the distance a couple other runners were visible, but there was no chance of closing the gap, which at that point was probably more than a mile. Still, it was reassuring to see them out there. As I finally reached the 15-mile mark and the course curved to the right, I knew the next mile marker would be one I had seen already. Checkpoint three at our original starting line was the next stop, and again I took the time to ingest enough nutrition to last the 6-mile trip along the backstretch of the triangle.

With only 11 miles to go, I had reached familiar territory. The 16-mile mark was real this time, but the miles were long and lonely. The only sound was the crunch, crunch, crunch as my feet pushed off the endless trail of crusty snow, passing one little red flag after another. Yet despite all the miles my body had experienced in the past twenty-five days, I felt great as I slowly traversed that 6-mile backstretch. Between miles 20 and 21, the final checkpoint came into view. I was doing math. 179 out of 184 miles of running were done. 5 miles to go. I tried to convert to Greenwich Mean Time so I could guess the net amount of time it had taken me to finish the continents. I estimated somewhere around 25 days and 18 hours. I only needed to stay vertical a little while longer.

Over forty years had passed since I sat in Bob Loesch's English class with a copy of the *Guinness Book of World Records* and dreamed of being a world record holder. In a few minutes, the dream would be a reality.

Before mile 24, I made my way around the curve that would take the course into camp and the finish line. The sun had made the snow a little softer the second time around, and I labored to make sure I had the best footing with each step. As I approached mile 25, some of the staff was a little ahead of schedule in preparing for the 100K race that would take place the next day, and they drove the big tractor with a sled behind it right onto the course ahead of me to re-groom the trail. That would have been fine, but when first groomed, it takes a few hours to firm up, so all they did for me was make the last mile more difficult. I was kicking up the freshly-loosened snow, so my shoes were covered as I hit the 25-mile mark. I saw the camp in the distance, slowly getting closer as I struggled to find good footing. Specks of color soon became tents and airplanes, and then people.

The people got larger and more defined as I approached the Antarctic Ice Marathon banner stretched across the finish line. At 7:10 p.m. I crossed the finish line with a time of 7:53:38. My old friend Richard Donovan was there to put my medal around my neck and give me a hug. One of my best friends, Brent Weigner, was there with a small bottle of Johnnie Walker Black whisky. New friends from the trip were there with handshakes and congratulations as well.

From the start in Soweto at 6:00 a.m. Johannesburg time (04:00 GMT) on November 6, the lapsed time was exactly 25 days, 18 hours, and ten minutes. A new world record.

The other runners were in the dining tent, and I joined them to warm up and dry off for a bit. We managed to consume a lot of food and the normal wine and beer that was always served with dinner. Participants had also brought special bottles for post-race celebration. As the remaining runners finished, we ran out to watch and congratulate them. Soon, all of us were celebrating our amazing adventure together.

A mountain shouldn't be considered climbed until you get back to the bottom. And an adventure isn't complete until it's shared with the people who matter the most. I left the celebration to take care of some unfinished business. I bought a half-hour of satellite phone time and called Francine. The people at home were already ahead of me. My daughter, Katie, had the Ice Marathon website on auto refresh, so as Richard called the results back to his brother and things were posted, everyone back home received updates from my daughter and my sister. Hundreds of people had already "Liked" the Facebook posts announcing to the world the news of my record. Reconnecting with Francine and sharing my success made it complete.

"I think what he does is good for inspiring other people," Francine said. "He says he's not an elite athlete and he doesn't run fast, but because of that, he can inspire everyday people to say, 'You know what, if this late-in-life "ordinary guy" runner can get out there and do it, I can do it too.'"

More than five years had passed since that day at the Bagel Beanery, but finally the record book would read:

MARATHON ON EACH CONTINENT - MEN

Donald Kern (USA) completed a marathon on each of the seven continents in 25 days, 18 hours, and 10 minutes between November 6 and December 1, 2011.

Chapter 16

and the adventure continues . . . .

A long time ago, I started signing my emails with the line "and the adventure continues ...." I'm not sure why, really, but it reminds me every time I sign out that life *is* an adventure. In everything I do, I try to make it like that.

Adventure. Where the result is uncertain. A bold undertaking. An exciting or unusual experience.

I catch myself sometimes, while hiking across a mountain ridge or running on a frozen ocean, laughing out loud at how cool my life is. "My friends are all back in Michigan at their desks, and here I am, hiking along a mountain ridge in Antarctica." What a kick! It's good to keep in mind that *that's* why we work. We get satisfaction while we work, but the real legacy we'll leave is the experiences we have and the stories we tell about them. Nobody, even the people you work with, will remember that you showed up for work like a good employee every day. We have to experience. We have to share. We have to leave a legacy. We have to be more than just a legend in our own mind.

Developing a sense of adventure makes life exciting. It keeps us motivated. Face it: We start out in life uncertain of the outcome. Life *is* adventure. Jump in.

Plan B

A couple years ago, Paul Ruesch sent me a text message on my birthday in May: "You want to run the marathon in Rio next month?"

"Sure," I said, as if there would be any other reply.

Game on. So after parking at Paul's place in Chicago and taking the train to O'Hare International Airport, we tried to check in for the flight. "You have a visa?" the ticket agent asked us. Two international travelers, and neither of us knew you needed a visa in advance to fly to Brazil. It's impossible to get one in less than about three business days. We were out of luck.

Maybe. "Hey, we need to *do something* this weekend to make up for this colossal screw-up. I have an idea.", I said to Paul.

Francine was running a marathon in Charlevoix, Michigan, the next morning. We called her from the train back to Paul's and told her to register us for the marathon. We were off on another adventure. From Chicago, we drove around Lake Michigan to Charlevoix, arriving at around 9 p.m., and the next morning, we ran the marathon. After a nice lunch, Paul and I got back in the van and headed north.

We had mid-afternoon beers at Legs Inn in Cross Village in the northern tip of the Lower Peninsula. After crossing the Mackinaw Bridge, we enjoyed a mid-afternoon snack of good old UP Pasties, then ate dinner that night at a brewery in Marquette. We went on to L'Anse, spent a short night in an inexpensive motel, and got up to climb Mount Arvon, Michigan's highest point, on Sunday morning. Back in L'Anse, we went to the beach and jumped in Lake Superior, where I swam a few strokes in my fourth of the five Great Lakes, checking off another of my Life List items.

Then it was on to Duluth, Minnesota, where we followed Lake Superior's coast northeast for about 90 miles, then another 20 miles north to the trailhead for Eagle Mountain, the highest point in Minnesota. After hiking the 6-mile round trip to the summit and providing the mosquitoes about a pint of blood each, we returned to Fitger's Brewery in Duluth just after they quit serving food. We still managed to collect a beer glass and enjoy a refreshing alcohol-enhanced beverage, then went out in search of a pizza before finding a place to drop for the night. Neither of us remember hitting a pillow that night.

On Monday afternoon, I dropped Paul off at his condo in Chicago and headed home. Our "massive screw-up" turned into us running a marathon, climbing two mountains, swimming in Lake Superior, visiting three breweries, and driving all the way around Lake Michigan. We exchanged our original airline tickets and ran a marathon in Costa Rica that September instead.

Don't be afraid to embrace your screw-ups. There's always a Plan B.

Turn Off the Filters

You probably noticed a few times that there wasn't much thinking between the times I heard about something and the time I signed up for them. The Antarctica Marathon, the Millennium Marathon, the South Pole Marathon, and the North Pole Marathon are a few adventures I've jumped into without taking the time to figure out why not. Sometimes you just have to step out and do something, and turn off that part of your brain that needs to think for hours before acting.

Incidentally, jumping in before looking can sometimes get one into more adventures than one bargained for. Keep a good sense of humor. You'll be fine, most of the time.

Living in the Moment

Traveling is great. Traveling without making reservations is much more exciting. I love climbing into a car and just going somewhere, figuring out what to do along the way. I was in Bismarck, North Dakota, for a marathon a few years ago without a hotel reservation, only to find out an Intertribal powwow had the whole town (and *every* hotel room) full of Native Americans. (Yes, that's right. The Indians had all the reservations.) So I bought a blanket and throw pillow at Wal-Mart and camped out in the back of my Subaru Outback rental car.

Putting yourself into situations is a great way to hone survival skills. I'm fond of saying, "I have a contingency plan. When I come to a contingency, I make a plan."

Fear

One of the best questions Mike asked me while we were working on this project is this: "What are you afraid of?" It reminded me of a conversation that happened one Saturday morning.

Early in 2011, I was talking with the lovely Francine's brother, Randy, at the family "happy hour" on a Friday evening when he told me about the Rev 3 Ironman-distance triathlon he had just signed up for. There were still open spots available. I managed to hold out until Tuesday before signing up. Then, as I keep telling people to do, I informed everybody I was doing it. (Friends have a way of making us either live up to our commitments or never letting us hear the end of it.)

A couple weeks later on a Saturday morning run from John Ball Park in Grand Rapids, a friend came up beside me and said, "I'm really proud of you."

"Thanks. What did I do?"

It was about signing up for the triathlon. Then she asked me a question that surprised me: "Aren't you afraid?"

"Huh?"

"What if you fail? What if you can't do it?"

Wow. I hadn't considered that. I suppose there was that possibility, but what if I did?

Truthfully, I've had things that didn't quite work out before. I tried to break the world record for running the seven continents twice and still hadn't done it. I was going to be a millionaire by the time I was 30. And 40. And 50. Maybe I'll make it by 60. But what if I fail?

Some people have questions like that going on in their minds when signing up for a marathon. There's a possibility you'll fail.

So what? What if you never even try?

Dealing with Fear

My friend, Christa, was going to run her first marathon a few years ago. I had referred her to the same hotel we were staying in, and when we went to her room, her fiancé answered the door. She was sitting on the bed with a pillow in her lap. Her head was buried in the pillow. She was crying.

There was too much stress and too many things to remember. All the advice, the coaching, the books, the words of the "experts" swirled around in her head. Combined with the next day's venture into the unknown, she was completely overwhelmed.

***

A few years earlier, I had jumped off a bridge in New Zealand. Don't worry. I was connected to a big rubber band. As I stepped off the platform into thin air, I discovered something in the next half-second. There was nothing I could do. Either I was going to die or I wasn't. After that, my mind totally changed modes, and I was focused on the experience, the fun, the adrenaline, the sensations. *It was great!*

***

I hugged Christa and shared the lesson I learned in that very short second in New Zealand: "Either you're ready or you're not. It's too late to worry about that now." All that advice echoing in her head was just extra noise. We went out to eat, relaxed, and enjoyed the moment. We met again at the starting line. She was still a little nervous, but enjoying the experience. On the out-and-back course, I saw her, still on her way out, 2 or 3 miles behind me as I was heading back. She was smiling. Enjoying. I crossed the road and gave her a big smooch. She was having a great time. I was having a great time.

Later, as she crossed the finish line, I grabbed a finisher medal from a race volunteer and put it around her neck. The tears of the day before were replaced with joy. Her first marathon.

So, I said all that to make this point:

RE-FREAKIN'-LAX

When that moment of truth comes, there's nothing more to be done than enjoy the moment. You can't prepare any more. You're as ready as you'll be. Have fun. Feel the energy of those around you, and encourage them. Absorb all the joy from it you can.

"What are you afraid of?"

Back to Mike's question. What if I got old and died before I had a chance to live? What if I'm sitting in a rocking chair someday without any really good stories to tell my great grandchildren? What if all I did was go to work for someone else and come home at night and mow my lawn and watch TV? What if I check out before I've even been here?

Now that's scary. I'm not going to do that.

My Theory of Evolution

For many millennia, the main purpose of life has been to reproduce itself, passing down the good qualities from one generation to the next. Generally, good genetic traits tend toward making life stronger, better, more fit for survival. However, those with less desirable traits tend to die out. "Survival of the fittest."

We've evolved over billions of years through natural selection, and small changes have accumulated so that we've slowly become the race of people we are today. I believe man has advanced beyond that now. We have the ability through technology and education to overcome many handicaps. The "fittest" now includes a lot more people. As a species, we've adapted our environment to our own purposes and gone far beyond our pure genetic code.

We've arrived at the next phase in our evolution. Instead of passing on our DNA, it's imperative that, as humans, we pass on those things that strengthen our species. Hope. Love. The spirit of adventure. Our consciousness drives the species forward faster than our DNA ever did.

It's probably inaccurate to say I'm always successful at advancing mankind. My "ideal self," however, strives to help everyone I come into contact with become a little better. While it may not always work, I hope the balance of my scale is substantially positive.

All of us can improve our species by affecting more than just our direct descendants. All of us can benefit by the attitude.

I hope my genetics represent an improvement for my kids and grandkids. But I'm certain that helping people set and achieve big goals will have a positive impact on the species for years to come. If I can help friends in Illinois start a new marathon, help finance a power wheelchair through working with Alternatives in Motion, or help kids go to the YMCA summer camp, it feels like success to me. It feels like I'm helping my fellow human beings. I like that.

What Does Something Like That Cost?

Sometimes people ask that. It isn't cheap traveling around the world, or even going somewhere for a weekend to run a marathon or climb a mountain.

Then again, I don't drive sports cars. My house is modest, I don't own a boat, and I don't smoke cigarettes. It's never been my habit to spend more than I make. Even when I travel, I'm fairly frugal.

I suspect part of the nature of the question is to provide the questioner with a graceful exit. "Oh, well, I could never afford something like that." If that's why you're asking, then any answer that includes a dollar amount would be a disservice.

So here's the real answer: What does it cost if you *don't* follow your dreams? Sitting in a rocking chair thinking about all the things you should have done. Could have done. That didn't cost you dollars. It cost you *life*.

What it costs is just a little more conviction, a little more planning, and a little more courage. Pay that cost, and you'll be sitting in your rocking chair remembering some pretty amazing stuff.

The Power of Faith

If the evolution discussion offended you earlier, maybe I can make up for it here.

Faith isn't a religious concept for me. Or maybe it is. I really think the whole concept of faith came about because of mankind's observation of how the world works. Maybe that's why it works for people in every religion, and even for atheists.

Have you noticed it seems like every time Jesus healed someone, he would say something like, "your faith has made you whole"?

There were a lot of instances like that, "As a man thinketh . . . " and that sort of thing. Even something like, "the Word became flesh and dwelt among us." Was that really a mystical thing, a human manifestation of God? Or was it someone long ago trying to get the point across that our words become our reality?

By this time, we should have realized that the thoughts we have inside our head are powerful forces in our lives. The words we put down on paper and use to communicate with one other soon take form in the outcome of our lives and the lives of those we influence.

It's time to believe in ourselves and make things happen.

You Don't Have to Be Superman

We're impressed by the Supermen in the news—guys like Michael Jordan, one of the best basketball players ever. Michael Phelps, who swims faster than fish and broke the record for Olympic gold medals. Usain Bolt, the speediest man on the planet. Justin Verlander, who routinely throws a fastball over 100 miles-an-hour. They're gifted athletes with a combination of natural abilities, the right parents to nurture them, the right timing, and the right opportunities.

Then there's you and me. We think we have to sit in the stands, wearing shirts with somebody else's name and number on them, rooting for college teams from schools we may have never attended. We just want to share in the glory.

It doesn't have to be that way. Ordinary people can do amazing things.

A few years back, I met Clyde Shank at a marathon in New Jersey. He was just back from Antarctica, so we had a lot to talk about. We've seen each other a few times since and became friends.

On May 1, 2012, Clyde posted on Facebook a thank you note to a couple friends for "hosting a wonderful 'Beer Tuesday' celebration in my honor of being the 4th person in the world to have run a marathon on all seven continents, the North Pole, and the 50 States."

Clyde had recently completed the North Pole Marathon. In his post, he pointed out something that hadn't occurred to me before. He was only the fourth person on earth to do that. I know the first three people. They're Brent Weigner, me, and Ginny Turner. In that order.

Clyde isn't a "Superman" type of person. Neither are Ginny or Brent. And me? You've read the stories.

Ordinary people can do amazing things.

Finding Your Passion

I had a nice conversation with a friend who ran his first marathon in Grand Rapids a couple years ago. He's doing well for a young man but was trying to figure out what he would do with his life at that moment.

Do with my advice as you will, but here's what I believe and what I told him: Creating a life list may be the closest any of us will ever get to creating life itself. As my own list grew, it seemed more and more like a living organism. Again, the goals meshed with one other, one complementing another, pulling me in along with them. I gave it life, and now it gives me life.

It's the quickest way to find your passion. Face it, we all need some basic things –a little cash flow to keep things together, necessities like food, clothing and shelter—but after that, it's a matter of figuring out what's really important to you. Doing that is the difference between just getting by and really living.

Spending the necessary time to put a hundred things on your list is critical. The first few are easy. But as you continue, you will have to dig inside your head and figure out what you really want. Before you're done, the picture emerges.

Got the basics covered? Then don't just go home after work and mow your lawn or watch TV. Spend the time working on the things you really want. Use that time to find your passion.

Start with your list and knock out an item here and there. Before long, you'll find you've got quite a résumé of accomplishments. Things that looked huge before have become routine.

Believe in Yourself

I think the reason guys like to watch an action movie is that we want to think of ourselves as superheroes. Strong, full of action, able to beat unbeatable odds. There's something to be said for that. Look in the mirror and tell yourself how strong, how capable, how good-looking, how successful you are. When people doubt you, give them an attitude that says, "Yeah, well stand back and watch this." There really is a Superman in each of us—and you don't even need a red cape.

And do your training, of course. It's part of the deal, and sometimes it hurts. If it were easy, it wouldn't feel nearly so rewarding when it's done.

The finisher medal, the diploma, the job you land—they're just tokens of your achievement. The real gift you receive for finishing is the knowledge that *you* can make a plan and complete a big goal. It's life-changing.

Back to my friend Andie's question: "What if you fail?" Really? Reframe the question. "What if it doesn't work the first time you try it?" You'll learn something about yourself. You'll benefit from the conditioning and find out how much more you need to do. You'll sign up for another event real soon and show the world the stuff you're made of.

Be fearless. Now stand back and watch this!

Epilogue

It's been a fun journey. One that frequently takes unexpected turns and, like life itself, mutates in unforeseeable ways. Let me share one last story.

It had been four years since the "Naked at the South Pole" incident when an interesting sequence of events happened.

In early February 2006, I went to renew my Michigan license plate and driver's license. Unfortunately, I was told that wasn't possible because my license was suspended—in Arizona. Yes, I was dinged for speeding there in 2001, but I had paid the ticket. Locating a canceled check from five years earlier wasn't going to happen, so I called The Grand Canyon State. After spending more than forty-five minutes on hold, I was told that $10 would clear up the situation. Pretty cheap. End of story, right?

A couple hours later, I received a phone call from the same Arizona area code. What now? This time, though, it was from Michelle Donati, who worked for a firm called Rose & Allyn Public Relations. They were producing an ad campaign and wanted to use a picture from my website. What picture? Remember the "naked at the South Pole" incident? "Your picture is exactly what we need for an ad we're producing."

I laughed and asked, "Okay, just what the hell are you trying to sell here?" It seems they were targeting lobbyists, with the idea that "there's no such thing as overexposure."

Michelle offered to pay $250 to use my picture, and I sent her the high-resolution copy from my computer. By now, you know I have a "Life List." Being a professional nude model wasn't on it, but what the heck?

Shortly after, the *Phoenix New Times* reprinted the picture, called me a "pasty white dude clad only in boots, a watch, and a beanie" in an article that claimed the newspaper had received "calls from a not-so-amused lobbyist." Everyone's a critic.

As if that weren't enough, around that same time, I received another email from Mick in the U.K. To say the least, it was interesting:

> "I am in the process of making a web site called nakedworldrecords.com and I would like to include your feat of standing naked at both poles. I would also like to use one of your photographs on my site. In return, I will offer you a free link to either your home page or a charity of your choice.
>
> By the way, can you tell me the date on which you stood naked at the second of the two poles, just in case someone wants to claim they did it earlier?"

When the page went live a couple weeks later, front and center on the home page was that same "pasty white dude." Last I checked, you can still find my smiling face on the homepage for nakedworldrecords. com. While my picture is modestly posed, it's probably not a good idea to visit the website at work.

Oh, the record date was April 18, 2003, by the way. Can anyone beat that?

Records Are Made to be Broken

In 2012, on my sixth trip to Antarctica, this time with Marathon Tours, I met Wendelin Lauxen from Germany. His shirt immediately gave away his goal; he was out to break my record. Unfortunately, he didn't make it on that attempt. A flight problem after we returned to the mainland kept him from getting to South Africa in time for the next marathon. He went on to break Richard Takata's record, but the world record was still mine.

I knew it wouldn't last. In November of 2012, we met again in Port Douglas, Australia, for the Solar Eclipse Marathon, which was conveniently on a Wednesday. On his second attempt, he was successful, completing the circuit in 21 days, 5 hours, and 33 minutes. We last saw each other on a particularly hard out-and-back section of the course, hugged each other, and wished each other well. I had done what I set out to do. It was his turn. He soon became the second person to finish all seven continents twice in a year.

The Life List

The life list continues to increase and decrease. In 2012, I checked off climbing Mount Katahdin in Maine and seeing Punxsutawney Phil on Groundhog Day in Pennsylvania.

My marathon days aren't over yet, but I've slowed down the schedule a bit. My at-least-once-a-month streak ended in April 2012 with some knee problems, but I was 8 months past the 100-month goal, so that was OK with me.

There are still a lot of things on the list that aren't nearly as strenuous that I'm working on. There are still nine U.S. state high points I haven't climbed and six states where I haven't yet collected a beer glass. Twenty states remain where I haven't run a marathon for the third time.

I still haven't run with the bulls or kissed the Blarney Stone.

I still want to ride a unicycle and learn to play the guitar.

I still haven't made a million dollars.

The next few years are full of possibilities. I'm looking forward to seeing great things, meeting good people, and having amazing experiences. Care to join me?

The List is alive. It grows more often than it shrinks. The marathon career may taper off, but there are still people to inspire, events to organize, and wonders to behold. Uncertain results and bold undertakings. Exciting and unusual experiences. I can't wait to see what happens next.

and the adventure continues . . . .

Where Are They Now?

You've met a few interesting people along the way. Here's a brief update on their whereabouts.

Brent Weigner continues his globetrotting exploits, recently finishing his eighth time running all seven continents and pretty much sticking me with no better than second place for the foreseeable future.

Paul Ruesch is still a sucker for adventure. After a three-year stint in the Peace Corps, he married Theyla from Mexico and is a proud dad of a beautiful daughter (and another one on the way). He and I are still sharing adventures, recently to the Solar Eclipse Marathon in Port Douglas, Australia, along with Theyla, Francine, and Brent and his wife, Sue Hume.

Richard Takata held the world record for over four years as I attempted it. Like the rest of us, he knew the record wouldn't last forever. He offered his congratulations and continues his pursuits raising money for Marathons for Wellness.

Richard Donovan still organizes the northernmost and the southernmost marathon races on the planet, and in February 2012, he broke his own world record for running the marathon distance (not necessarily in organized marathon events) on all seven continents in 4 days, 22 hours, 3 minutes.

John Bozung, the guy I credit with planting the seven continents idea in my head, has the currently active streak for the most consecutive months running a marathon. His streak stretches a bit over 20 years right now.

Francine Robinson, better known to the readers of my regular email newsletter as "The Lovely Francine," is my partner in life. She's also a strong marathon runner, has two beautiful daughters, and trains other runners through the mentor program with the Grand Rapids Running Club.

Shawn Sweet, my old partner-in-race instigation, lives in paradise on the island of Oahu with his wife Joyce. He works for Delta Airlines but spends most of his time enjoying all that the tropical environment has to offer. He recently came out of running retirement and ran the Honolulu Marathon.

Marcus Fillinger, the North Pole SCUBA diver, runs Alpha Dog Ranch, an animal rescue operation in Australia. He's a strong advocate for animal rights.

Ed Kornoelje, Director of Sports Medicine at Metro Health, is the doctor most likely to keep an athlete in the game. Since setting up a M.A.S.H.-unit-style medical tent at the first Grand Rapids Marathon, he became a multiple marathon runner himself. He's still my doctor.

Terence Reuben, who told me "You might have a torn meniscus," is the most sought-after physical therapist in Grand Rapids. He is a founding member of My Team Triumph, a charity that helps people with disabilities participate in major sporting events. He's also completed the Ironman Triathlon a couple times, as well as the Comrades Marathon in South Africa.

Dr. Peter Theut, knee surgeon, is still fixing knees and other joints in Grand Rapids, Michigan.

Dean Karnazes, the only supermodel I've ever shared a room with, has become the premier ultra-distance running missionary. With books *Ultramarathon Man*, *50/50*, and *RUN!*, and a mission to combat childhood obesity through his "No Child Left Inside" program, he inspires runners all over the world. He still doesn't have any body fat.

Bean Bowers, whose level head and outdoor experience helped keep us safe on the way to the South Pole, died on July 10, 2011, after a two-year battle with brain cancer. He was 38. On his memorial page, I posted, "I'm just a snow melter," you said when we were introduced at the Punta Arenas airport in 2002, en route to the South Pole. Over the next month, you helped keep us safe and became a good friend. Level head, great ability, great sense of humor. We haven't kept in touch much, but I will miss you. Guide on, my friend.

Dave Sheble, Co-Race Director of the Fox Valley Marathon with Craig Bixler, continues to spread the word. Dave, Craig and a host of other great organizers, have now started a new marathon in Naperville, Illinois, which will be run for the first time in November 2013.

Dr. William Tan, who holds the world record for running all seven continents in a wheelchair, sent me an update: "My Patriot Hills attempt was actually my third attempt at the seven-continents undertaking—after which I was diagnosed with stage IV (end stage) chronic lymphocytic leukemia. Since then, I have been battling with chemotherapy and bone marrow transplant; my oncologist thinks I already had leukemia when I started my first attempt in 2005, since the medical texts document that the progress from stage I to stage IV takes ten years." William inspires others even as he works through his own challenges. He still looks forward to a return to marathoning.

Nasreen Fynewever, who shared my adventures with her classes and encouraged them to dream, declares she will be a teacher for life—at times in the classroom and at other times with whomever she meets. She has added "writer" and "speaker" to the mix and finds ways to champion other people's dreams and causes. She is a hope chaser.

Mary Ritz, my North Pole travel companion, is another person I've run with and drunk with on every continent. She recently retired from her job as park ranger in Wyoming. Our most recent adventure together was a marathon in a torrential downpour in Roanoke, Virginia. In June, 2013, she became the fifth person on earth to run marathons in all 50 states, all seven continents, and the North Pole.

Lauraine Kern Emmons, my little sister, who wanted me to bring a rock home from the North Pole, was always my biggest fan. Before I could call home she had already informed most of the free world the day I broke the world record. While I was finishing the final edits of this book, she had a stroke and is no longer with us. She has the first autographed manuscript of this book with her forever. Lauraine Kern Emmons, May 7, 1960 – May 17, 2013.

And my mom, Julaine Kern, is still alive and well and living in Barryton, Michigan. She still knows better than to tell me I can't do something.